● REC

# CAPTURING
## THE CLASSROOM

*Creating Videos to Reach*
*Students Anytime*

# ELLEN I. LINNIHAN

Solution Tree | Press
a division of
Solution Tree

555 North Morton Street
Bloomington, IN 47404
800.733.6786 (toll free) / 812.336.7700
FAX: 812.336.7790

email: info@SolutionTree.com

Visit **go.SolutionTree.com/technology** to download the free reproducibles in this book.

Printed in the United States of America

Library of Congress Cataloging-in-Publication Data

Names: Linnihan, Ellen, author.
Title: Capturing the classroom : creating videos to reach students anytime
  / Ellen I. Linnihan.
Description: Bloomington, IN : Solution Tree Press, 2021. | Includes
  bibliographical references and index.
Identifiers: LCCN 2021014251 (print) | LCCN 2021014252 (ebook) | ISBN
  9781952812057 (paperback) | ISBN 9781952812064 (ebook)
Subjects: LCSH: Interactive videos--Planning. | Video
  recordings--Production and direction. | Video tapes in education.
Classification: LCC LB1028.75 .L56 2021  (print) | LCC LB1028.75  (ebook) |
  DDC 371.33/467--dc23
LC record available at https://lccn.loc.gov/2021014251
LC ebook record available at https://lccn.loc.gov/2021014252

**Solution Tree**
Jeffrey C. Jones, CEO
Edmund M. Ackerman, President

**Solution Tree Press**
*President and Publisher:* Douglas M. Rife
*Associate Publisher:* Sarah Payne-Mills
*Art Director:* Rian Anderson
*Managing Production Editor:* Kendra Slayton
*Copy Chief:* Jessi Finn
*Senior Production Editor:* Tonya Maddox Cupp
*Content Development Specialist:* Amy Rubenstein
*Copy Editor:* Mark Hain
*Proofreader:* Sarah Ludwig
*Text Designer:* Abigail Bowen
*Editorial Assistants:* Sarah Ludwig and Elijah Oates

# DEDICATION

This book is dedicated to Team Linnihan, who has supported me through every step of my journey—both teaching and writing. To my husband, Patrick, whose dreams know no limits. He inspires confidence when I need moral support and always helps me see the big picture. To my children, Madison and Sean, whose creativity are so far out of the box that they never knew there *was* a box. To my children, Ryan and Michael, who continue to push me to learn and grow with the times, challenging me and helping me learn anything related to technology. To my dogs, who missed more than just a couple of walks throughout the course of this journey but faithfully slept at my feet through it all. To my students, who sparked the light. To my father, Richard Schmitz, who did not live to see the book in print, but continues to live on in my heart.

Solution Tree Press would like to thank the following reviewers:

Jennifer Brown
Instructional Coach
Annandale High School
Annandale, Virginia

Tracey Eatherton
Family and Consumer
    Sciences Teacher
Ste. Genevieve High School
Ste. Genevieve, Missouri

Alexander Fangman
Principal
Grant's Lick Elementary School
Alexandria, Kentucky

Lisa Johnson
Educational Technologist
Westlake High School
Austin, Texas

Scott Spoede
Assistant Principal
Chipeta Elementary School
Grand Junction, Colorado

Anthony Stamm
Curriculum Coordinator
Ann Arbor Public Schools
Ann Arbor, Michigan

Ariane Richard Tuomy
Curriculum and Career
    Education Facilitator
Palo Alto Unified School District
Palo Alto, California

Kristal Vallie
English Language Arts Teacher
Bussey Middle School
Garland, Texas

Visit **go.SolutionTree.com/technology** to download
the free reproducibles in this book.

# TABLE OF CONTENTS

About the Author. . . . . . . . . . . . . . . . . . . . vii

Introduction . . . . . . . . . . . . . . . . . . . . . .1

    The Why and How of Videos and Archives . . . . . . . . 4

    Benefits for Students. . . . . . . . . . . . . . . . 5

    Benefits for Teachers. . . . . . . . . . . . . . . . 14

    About This Book . . . . . . . . . . . . . . . . . . 21

*Chapter 1*
**Creating a Diverse Archive Throughout the School Year . . . 23**

    Recording Different Types of Videos . . . . . . . . . 24

    Recording Specific Subjects and Approaches . . . . . . 42

    Using Video for Professional Growth. . . . . . . . . . 49

    Try This . . . . . . . . . . . . . . . . . . . . . 50

    Conclusion . . . . . . . . . . . . . . . . . . . . 51

*Chapter 2*
**Preparing Before the Students Arrive . . . . . . . . . . . 53**

    Get Permission From Administration . . . . . . . . . . 54

    Start With a Checklist . . . . . . . . . . . . . . . 56

    Set Up Your Communication Platform. . . . . . . . . . 58

    Choose and Set Up Your Video-Hosting Platform. . . . . 61

    Set Up an FAQ . . . . . . . . . . . . . . . . . . 61

    Communicate With Students, Parents, and Guardians . . 63

    Gather Your Equipment and Prepare Technology . . . . . 71

Lay the Groundwork for an Archive . . . . . . . . . . . 75

Try This . . . . . . . . . . . . . . . . . . . . 83

Conclusion . . . . . . . . . . . . . . . . . . . 84

*Chapter 3*
**Building Communication Confidence** . . . . . . . . . . . . **85**
Build Confidence for Teachers . . . . . . . . . . . . 85

Build Confidence for Students . . . . . . . . . . . . 99

Try This . . . . . . . . . . . . . . . . . . . . 111

Conclusion . . . . . . . . . . . . . . . . . . . 113

**Epilogue.** . . . . . . . . . . . . . . . . . . . . . **115**

**References and Resources** . . . . . . . . . . . . . . **117**

**Index** . . . . . . . . . . . . . . . . . . . . . . . **125**

# ABOUT THE AUTHOR

 **Ellen I. Linnihan** is a secondary English and public speaking teacher in the Elmbrook School District in Brookfield, Wisconsin. She is also an adjunct faculty member for the University of Wisconsin-Oshkosh Cooperative Academic Partnership Program (CAPP). Linnihan began her career teaching in Department of Defense schools in Kentucky and California. While raising four children, she spent ten years as a freelance writer for educational publishing companies. She has been cultivating an archive of teaching videos since 2015 and is a strong advocate of including all learners in her classroom, whether they are face-to-face, remote, or hybrid learners.

Linnihan earned her National Board Certification for teaching secondary English in 2018. It was this experience that ignited a passion for sharing her ideas about creating a video archive to better serve her students. In addition to teaching, Linnihan is the program coordinator for the Distinguished Young Women of Brookfield scholarship program, a national program that develops and recognizes academic achievement, talent, and leadership in young women. She credits this program for launching her in a positive direction in life when she was a high school participant. In 2020, she was selected as one of the most influential educators for the Elmbrook School District.

Linnihan earned her bachelor's degree in English and history from the University of Wisconsin-Madison. She furthered her studies at Austin Peay State University with a master's degree in education (curriculum and instruction) and a master's degree in English.

To learn more about Ellen's work, visit @EllenLinnihan on Twitter, ellenlinni on Instagram, or www.capturingtheclassroom.com.

To book Ellen I. Linnihan for professional development, contact pd@SolutionTree.com.

# INTRODUCTION

My inspiration to create a video archive was born of necessity. As a lifelong lover of word games and puzzles, I tend to look at life with the goal of a satisfying win. Like a puzzle with the picture on the cover, I have a vision for what my students should accomplish while in my classroom. Anything short of this feels like a puzzle with missing pieces. While students don't always fully complete the puzzle in my class, I do my best to ensure that they have the pieces they need to do so. At one point I realized that the students sitting in my classroom had all the pieces, but that students who were absent did not. This inspired me to begin building a video archive.

In 2015, on the first day of the start of a new high school term, a guidance counselor contacted me to let me know I would have a student, Grant, starting my class who had a unique situation. Grant had been homebound for the past year due to cancer treatments but was finally ready to jump back into his public education. The catch? It was January in Wisconsin, and the schools were undoubtedly plagued by nasty viruses. For most, this kind of thing is a routine annoyance (unlike the 2020 COVID-19 pandemic that would follow a few years later), but it was a deadly matter for Grant. He would not be able to attend school physically for two months—eight weeks of the nine-week term. I immediately flashed back to John Travolta's 1976 hit made-for-television movie, *The Boy in the Plastic Bubble* (Thurm, Dunne, & Kleiser, 1976). I remembered the heartbreaking injustice of his situation. The teen heartthrob was compelled to live in a plastic enclosure because of a damaged immune system, unable to interact physically with the outside world. In thirty years, had we not progressed beyond isolation? While a solution did not immediately come to my mind, my gut instinct was, "Yes! We can do better than a plastic bubble for our students."

My first thought was to reach out to Grant through FaceTime, a video-communications app common to Apple devices. As my new class filed in on the first day, they were typical tenth-grade honors students on the surface. They sized each other up and selected seats, probably thinking that this would be just like any other class. In some ways, it turned out to be exactly true, and that was exactly my goal. I wanted this experience for Grant to be just as good, if not *better*, than it would be for any other student. But Grant was not going to join our class in eight weeks. *He was joining us that day.*

Even though it was the first day of the term, I am certain that Grant did not anticipate any immediate contact from me, but I wanted to make it work. Without any prior warning (I hadn't gotten any either), I decided to make contact during the class period. One student called Grant on his phone as the rest of us waited. Keep in mind that this was before Zoom was common in classrooms. We might have been making the first phone call in the history of the world for as much anticipation coursed through the air. Grant answered and was obviously caught off guard. His classmate explained that he was in his English language arts (ELA) class and that the teacher wanted him to FaceTime to join the class. After a brief pause, the in-class student hung up and laughed, "He needs a minute to change out of his pajamas!"

From then on, daily accommodations ensured that Grant was always fully included in the classroom experience. I checked out an extra laptop from the school library and dedicated it to connecting with Grant through Google Meet. The same student who had volunteered to call Grant on that first day of class took charge of making the daily connection for the call on the laptop. He simply moved the computer around the classroom, ensuring Grant could see instruction and remain actively involved. If we were doing group work, Grant's computer was sitting on a desk facing his group members. If he was speaking to the full class, his computer was on the podium, facing the students. I made sure that he had physical copies of classroom materials ahead of time and shared handouts and quizzes with him through email. As long as he had enough time to receive printed materials prior to class, everything ran very smoothly.

Grant's connection to the class was palpable, and our homebound mindset shifted radically. He didn't need a stack of busywork materials to justify completing the course. He needed the actual materials for this specific course. He was a part of the class, and providing him with anything less than the full experience would be like giving him a five hundred-piece puzzle with only four hundred pieces in the box. First, that would be a ridiculous challenge, but significantly, it would be meaningless and unfulfilling. This led to recording class periods when Grant was unable to join us in real time.

The reality of Grant's situation was that as much as we wanted him to be an integral member of the class, just like everyone else, there *was* something different about him. Yes, he was at home, and we were all in the classroom, but that was not the biggest difference. Grant had cancer. That meant tests, procedures, and hospital stays. There were days when he was not able to join us in real time, so recording class was critical to keeping him connected to us. He could watch class when he was home and felt well enough to do so.

A few weeks into the term with Grant's class, another student in his class approached me with a request that I record and share a daily class period video recording with her because she was going to be absent due to a field trip. Why not record classes for everyone?

Creating a video archive meant I was no longer confined by my classroom walls. Old boundaries that had dictated my effectiveness had burst like a bubble, and I would never again allow a student of mine to be trapped in a situation that would hinder his or her creativity or learning. This moment effectively laid the groundwork for recording my classroom instruction and customized tutorials. The archive developed organically through trial and error and a lot of video replacement. I found myself discovering new ways to use video to enhance my teaching through tutorials, lessons, and daily updates for both students and parents.

I taught for more than a decade without video, and I can recall many times when I thought to myself, "Did I already tell this class about X, or did I tell the other class last semester?" With a video archive, you will always know the answer to this question. If it's in the archive, the students have the information. If they had it last semester, you can rest assured that they have it this semester, too. Of course, you still teach students in real time, but having an archive of tutorials to supplement review ensures that students have access to the best and most thorough lessons you have to offer. Students can access the tutorials anytime to learn, reinforce, and review specific lessons.

You can record lectures, classroom discussions, assignment and technical tutorials, review sessions, and student presentations—basically, anything that happens in school (whether a physical classroom, virtual classroom, home office, or hybrid). The greatest benefit of creating and maintaining a video archive is the access it provides to learners outside the physical boundaries and specified time periods.

There are three basic steps to creating a video archive—a collection of recordings collected and stored on the internet intended to facilitate improved access and learning of classroom content.

1. **Record** (and possibly stream) daily lessons of live lectures, activities, tutorials, discussions, and so on.

2. **Archive** the recordings for future use.

3. **Share** access to the videos.

Yes, the concept is simple. But starting a new endeavor can be tough, and you may not feel fully comfortable with the technology. Don't worry—we'll get through this together! I'll provide the checklists and steps you need to start recording and archiving, as well as using videos to assess your own instruction and your peers'. It's the substance you are recording—*instruction*—that is the key to the success of this practice. A video archive essentially clones your teaching, and sharing videos maximizes your teaching potential. This introduction explains in more depth the why and how of videos and archives, as well as lays out the benefits for students and for teachers of these practices. Finally, I'll go into details about this book's organization.

## The Why and How of Videos and Archives

In this book, I write about why and how K–12 teachers can establish, organize, share, and maintain a video archive to support any content area or curriculum. While many teachers have figured out the basics of going virtual due to the COVID-19 pandemic, the intention of archiving is not survival. Creating an archive allows you to teach to the future, not just to the present. For example, I was able to provide prerecorded lessons for my students when two major back-to-back family emergencies forced me to miss the last ten days of the term. In addition, my colleagues did not need to scramble to create lessons for my classes.

This book advocates for why it is in your best interest and in your students' best interests to create a video archive. I am certainly not the first person to emphasize the *why* as the most essential point of a new idea. In fact, inspirational speaker Simon Sinek (2009) states, "People don't buy what you do; they buy why you do it. And what you do simply proves what you believe" (p. 41). My *why* is simple: creating a video archive will improve both teaching and learning.

While I will guide you through the logistics, this book is not a complicated how-to because there are a lot of platforms, and they are ever-changing. Such instructions could be out of date very soon. You don't need extensive technology skills to implement this strategy. Searching the internet for platform-specific steps should provide the details you need in the latest iteration of the technology. For example, when I started archiving, Zoom was not common in school. I did not have a camera set up in my classroom to automatically connect to the desktop and stream live lessons. Someday these devices may also be outdated, but I will adapt and use the newest technology as it evolves.

You are already teaching. Why not make the most of it? This approach breaks down physical barriers to facilitate real accessibility for students who are absent or who utilize distance learning part- or full-time. Similar to a flipped classroom, where students watch recorded instruction on their own time and use classroom time to do assignments, labs, and other tasks with the teacher present, with this approach you can provide instructional videos for students and their support networks to watch on their own time to learn and better comprehend the material. Support networks can be anyone with a vested interest in helping a student: parents, guardians, tutors, aids, special education teachers, paraprofessionals, and so on. It is easy to include anyone who wants to help by simply sharing a link.

Unlike a flipped classroom, in which the teacher works in isolation and has students prepare for the classroom on their own, *Capturing the Classroom* advises you to record your actual class periods when you're with students (in class, virtually, or both), save the videos to a shared online platform, and add videos throughout each year to build a robust archive of resources so your students and colleagues can easily access them. I also recommend creating and archiving other types of instruction. For complex material or multistep projects, as an example, you can record brief tutorials outside of regular class to provide additional support for students. A video archive does not replace traditional instruction. It enhances and reinforces it. For example, if you traditionally provide written instructions for an assignment, add a hyperlink to a video in the document so students can access the information in both text and video format. Video instructions may be more appealing to auditory learners, as well as those students with attention deficit hyperactivity disorder (ADHD) and autism (Aken, 2020; Ellison & Brdar, 2019). Providing multiple modalities increases the likelihood that students will take in the information and process it.

## Benefits for Students

A video archive of classroom lessons can benefit students in a variety of ways. Access to videos can reduce the stress a student may feel when preparing for or returning from an absence. Because there are many types of videos that you can record and provide, you can custom fit content for any given situation. For example, a recording of a previous class of students discussing the same chapter of a book serves for an occasional or emergency absence for a student or teacher. On the other hand, if a student has an extended absence, you may choose to stream and record the current class so that the missing student can connect with both the material and the actual students in the class. If you want to ensure a missing student feels connected to the full classroom experience, for example, you can shoot videos of the full room rather than a close-up of yourself. There is more than one way to approach recording. Some situations call for a tight shot of a teacher's hands when demonstrating something physical. Others may call for a roaming camera to capture various small-group activities. You may even find that recording the same lesson more than once from different angles and perspectives will offer multiple benefits for learners, depending on their needs and learning styles. Just keep in mind that there is not just one way to do something. *Any* video is better than *no* video, so try what you think will work. If it doesn't capture what you hoped, do it again!

Students can use videos as a primary learning source when absent or a review source when preparing for assessments. Both students who need extra reinforcement and students who are ready for faster content delivery can access videos and play them back at a speed that suits their learning style. For example, most streaming video services let users adjust playback speed to suit their preference. Just as reading speeds vary from one individual to the next, so too do listening and viewing speeds. Based on the situation, students may adjust as needed. When processing information for the first time, a student may choose the "normal" playback speed. For difficult material, a student may find it beneficial to slow the video (or pause occasionally, back up, and listen again to a specific portion to process the information). In contrast, if students are reviewing, they may find it beneficial to refresh the information quickly at a faster speed.

Students seeking out these videos also reinforces a core social-emotional skill: self-management (Weissberg, Durlak, Domitrovich, & Gullotta, 2015). Self-management boils down to students answering two questions: (1) "What different responses can I have to an event?" and (2) "How can I respond to an event as constructively as possible?" (Vega, 2017). Students can enact their self-management skills by using video to perform the following actions.

- Adjust instruction speed to fit individual need
- Get more equitable access for attention deficit hyperactivity disorder and autism
- Access interactive study tools
- Review content and prepare for assessments
- Access material missed due to absence
- Be included if homebound or requiring extended absence
- Improve public speaking and communication skills
- Bolster remote teaching and learning

The following sections explore each of these actions.

## *Adjust Instruction Speed to Fit Individual Need*

Most people can relate to the feeling that something is just over their head. It can take time for something to sink into our brains, and for many learners, slowing down may be the key to putting the pieces together. Whether students are tackling a mathematics equation, a scientific theory, or a poetry analysis, slowing down to process the information can make all the difference in comprehending a complex concept. In fact, "when we have more time to process information, the quality of our thinking and learning improves" (Jennings, 2015, as cited in MindShift, 2015). In addition, people process information at different speeds—elementary students especially need more processing time—and some process visual information more quickly than auditory information (Jennings, 2015). Being able to slow down, pause, and replay instructional recordings allows customized speed and variable input modes to meet students' needs. As long as students comprehend the topic in the end, the amount of time they spent travelling to that moment is irrelevant.

Using a video archive as a form of scaffolding meets students where they are without making additional work for you or delaying other students. Some students need more reinforcement than others. Some take longer to process information, while others seem to read your mind and can't wait for the starting cue. Using video is a natural way to scaffold lessons to meet student needs. For example, when teaching a skill that requires multiple steps—solving complicated equations, doing research—tutorial videos help keep everyone on track as they move through the process. You will still share traditional materials with directions for each step, but in this case, you can also hyperlink tutorial videos on the directions. If students are struggling to find online sources about a topic, they can watch a quick tutorial on how to do a more refined search. Other students may breeze right past this step because their search provided what they needed. Taking class time to address everyone at once for a problem that they may not be experiencing is disruptive.

Just as a video archive is useful for those students who may need repetition and a slower pace, students who become restless when content is delivered at a pace they consider too slow can speed up the video by adjusting the playback speed. While increasing speed is not necessarily advisable for all students, some find instruction more engaging at a faster pace. If the students are accessing the information to supplement learning based on their own desire for improvement, there is no great concern that they may abuse the opportunity by playing the videos faster than will benefit them. If they are seeking guidance or further information, they will do so naturally, and they can set the perfect pace for themselves.

What about issues that stump a lot of students? One example is questions about very specific auto-formatting issues in Word documents. When a lot of students run into a particular issue, direct them to a specific minute or second if you know where it is tackled in a video. You will likely be so familiar with the content that you can direct them to exactly what they need. For every student whose question is covered in video, that is a minute of your time spent on more in-depth content coverage or teaching students skills. The more frequently asked questions that you address with tutorials, the more time you save.

Additionally, a video archive addresses enrichment. Students who are already proficient can benefit from accessing supplemental or enhancement units that they can enjoy at their own pace.

**TEACHER** VOICES

[Video has] allowed me to connect with students who process a little slower and need the additional support when I can't help one-on-one.

—**Mike Carini, high school mathematics and technology teacher**

### *Get More Equitable Access for Attention Deficit Hyperactivity Disorder and Autism*

Equity in the classroom is every teacher's goal, but it is a challenge. Needs and ability levels vary widely. In fact, "as much as ninety-five percent of teachers have students with learning disabilities in their classroom" (Aken, 2020). A one-size-fits-all approach to teaching is a disservice to everyone.

A student may benefit from a different instructional delivery. Video can supplement and enhance classroom teaching for students who have different sensory needs, such as those with ADHD or autism. Besides the ability to somewhat set the pace, a video does the following (Aken, 2020).

- Lets students control stimuli
- Provides instant and high-speed feedback
- Draws attention with sounds and bright colors (if you provide them)
- Offers engaging interactive aspects (if you provide them)

When I was a child, I hated watching the news on TV because it was boring. The stoic person on the screen using uninteresting words in a monotone generated no excitement or interest in me. If you flip on a news station today, you will see a radically different approach than the one I recall from my youth. There are graphics splashed across the screen, and the colors are bright and engaging. The right amount of stimulation is engaging, but it is especially helpful for students who have ADHD (Aken, 2020). While some videos will be straightforward, the potential to do more exists. With programs such as Screencast-O-Matic (https://screencast-o-matic.com), you can add graphics, bright colors, pictures, music, and video clips to maximize viewer engagement. And you are not bound to the front of the classroom, either. You can record outside, for example, or just insert a fun graphic background.

## Access Interactive Study Tools

While you might opt for recording only classroom lectures or activities, you can explore making videos interactive. Research shows that "educational videos are most effective when they incorporate active-learning strategies such as asking students to pause videos and answer questions before proceeding with watching the rest of the video" (Pulukuri & Abrams, 2020). Interactivity can also be something like a clock to indicate time left to work on a task. And rest assured your presence is important: "Students appear to find videos which include the instructor's image to be more engaging, or they engage more with course content as a result of instructor presence in video" (Carmichael, Reid, & Karpicke, n.d.). You are still the key to classroom effectiveness.

## Review Content and Prepare for Assessments

Meeting the needs of all students in a classroom is the logical goal of any dedicated teacher. Goals and reality do not always align easily, however. Some students need extra support and repetition of key ideas. While the addition of paraprofessionals and parent volunteers can be helpful, many students could benefit from one more level of support. Having a video archive of the content allows each of these helpers to have eyes on the classroom material. Rather than asking a student, "What did you do in class today?," anyone in a student's support network—paraprofessionals, parents, tutors—can say, "Let's take a look at what you did in class today to see if you have any questions." Barak Rosenshine (2012), emeritus professor of educational psychology, confirms that all students benefit from weekly and monthly reviews of classroom material. Students can break down difficult concepts at a slower pace and review them with a support person or peer for better comprehension.

Some students find that by the time the unit test or summative assessment rolls around, they have forgotten some of what was covered earlier. A video archive is an excellent tool for students to prepare for an assessment. The ability to control the speed is, again, a valuable feature.

## *Access Material Missed Due to Absence*

Student absences are inevitable. Whether due to illness, field trips, vacations, or early dismissal for activities, attendance remains one of the greatest disruptors in education, as research shows. Research also shows that attendance is key to success: "Missing school has a distinct negative influence on performance, even after the potential mediating influence of other factors is taken into account, and this is true at all rates of absenteeism" (García & Weiss, 2018). Chronic absence, defined as missing 10 percent of school or more, is "one of the strongest and most often overlooked indicators of a student's risk of becoming disengaged, failing courses, and eventually dropping out of school" (Sparks, 2010, p. 1). Equity plays a role in absenteeism. Those students who are already at higher risk academically—those with a disability, who are eligible for free and reduced lunch, Hispanic English learners, and Native Americans—are most likely to have been absent (National Assessment of Educational Progress, 2015, as cited in García & Weiss, 2018).

Absences can impact a student's feeling of connectedness to the class. Research shows that "social isolation is associated with increased risk of cognitive decline and dementia, as well as mental health consequences such as depression and anxiety" (Offord, 2020). Whether physically absent or just mentally lost, having a sense that the class has moved on without you leads to feelings of confusion, isolation, and possibly even rejection from the group.

Consequently, every teacher has had to figure out how to get a student caught up after missing class—often several days' worth of material. For example, research indicates that 20 percent of eighth graders in the U.S. are chronically absent (García & Weiss, 2018). Some students return feeling overwhelmed and anxious about being behind. The teacher immediately faces a dilemma: conference one-to-one with the returning student or begin class as planned, leaving the returning student in the dark. Many teachers remove the student from the class (to the hall or to the side to do busywork), further delaying the student's successful return and engagement in the activities. It's important to remember that "to learn at high levels, students must have access to essential grade-level curriculum each year" (Buffum, Mattos, & Malone, 2018, p. 7).

> Videos catch you up to speed and make you feel as if you didn't miss a lesson at all. Watching them can be time-consuming, but it's so much better than other teachers who just throw you in the ocean and tell you to figure out how to swim.
>
> **—Tenth-grade student**

**STUDENT**
VOICES

> [Recording classes] has given me the freedom from having to repeat a lesson numerous times when a student has been absent or is behind.
>
> **—Christine Capriolo, high school art teacher**

**TEACHER**
VOICES

With a video archive, this scenario becomes nearly unnecessary. Granted, there will be times when students need additional guidance for reentry to the curriculum, but instructional videos will reduce the time it takes to get the student back on track. Students with access to video content for the missed days can catch up at home and return to class without missing a beat. When they do return, the teacher need only ask if they watched the videos and answer any questions students may have about the material. Having students access the videos on their own for absences also shifts the responsibility for the learning to the student, and the "ability to manage one's learning," according to researchers Kristina Zeiser, Carrie Scholz, and Victoria Cirks (2018), "can have significant effects on academic achievement" (p. 1). That makes such agency an important part of crucial soft skills, including self- and time management. You can create a Google Form or send a quick survey to ask students for their date of absence, whether they watched the video linked to that day's lesson, and what questions they have after watching it.

Even if students know they will be gone because of an exciting upcoming competition, field trip, or other big event, the stress of worrying about what they will miss often casts a shadow over the event. Whether they are heading to swim at nationals for a week, performing with the marching band at Disney World, or going to India for a family wedding, taking time away from classes can be a nightmare on return. Some students will let everything snowball and ignore the reality until returning to school. With a video archive, students can take action before they even pack their suitcases, working ahead prior to the absence and asking questions about materials before leaving. If they are working from afar, they can stay on pace with the class, emailing questions as they go through the coursework. Some students may still leave all the work for when they return, but providing this chance to exhibit agency and practice self-management skills is important (Zeiser et al., 2018).

Students are not the only ones who feel overwhelmed when missing school. Teachers feel it, too. Using a video archive to supplement teacher absences may positively affect both the teachers' and the students' mental health and success. Because "teachers are the most important school-based determinant of students' academic success [it's] no surprise researchers find that teacher absence lowers student achievement" (Miller, 2012). Simulating your presence with prerecorded lessons in a classroom setting is the closest duplication possible to your physical presence.

### *Be Included if Homebound or Requiring Extended Absence*

What if a student has to be at home for an extended amount of time? Humans are social by nature, and long absences can be detrimental to students' well-being (Terada, 2020). Consider this:

> *Social connection is defined as the interpersonal and interdependent closeness between people, resulting in a sense of belonging. Notably, it is not the number of or proximity to friends, or the frequency of interactions with others. Rather, social connection expresses the positivity and closeness that an individual perceives in their interactions with others. (Chuter, n.d.)*

Students need contact with their peers and teachers, and if educators care about both the physical and mental well-being of each other, we must address this fundamental human need for students who are physically unable to join their peers in the classroom. Videos can help break down the walls that can make students feel isolated (whether due to illness, extracurriculars, family needs, or displacement emergencies) and help keep all students on track for success.

Even though the teacher does not experience every teaching moment with pupils as they access the videos, students are still learning from the teacher, attaining a connection and a feeling of inclusion. When homebound or absent students watch classroom videos, whether streamed live or archived afterward, they see the other students and learn about them as well. Similar to how people begin to feel a personal connection with an actor on a favorite show or movie, the students may forge a bond with the teacher through the videos. Remember that video is not the only teaching method you are using. Videos are a great springboard for subsequent discussions. Just as you may enjoy rehashing a new release with friends, you have a perfect opportunity to do the same with your students regarding the video they watched. Answering questions incorporates the video in a meaningful way in the classroom, giving the students an opportunity to interact with you about the material.

If students watch a recording that includes students in the classroom, they benefit from the interactions and questions that the recorded students have. In this way, the live audience on the recording can provide a more natural experience for the viewers. Obviously, if the recording is of their actual classmates, the sense of inclusion will be greater.

## *Improve Public Speaking and Communication Skills*

There are benefits of improving public speaking through video. Seeing recordings of their presentations and others' and hearing what they sound like when trying to make a point are great ways to get students thinking about how to improve their skills in a general way (versus in a formal speech class).

Communication is fundamental to human experience. If we teach with a mindset to prepare our students to live as functioning members of society, the time to start practicing effective communication is now. Great communicators advocate for this philosophy. Dale Carnegie (1962) states, "There are four ways, and only four ways, in which we have contact with the world. We are evaluated and classified by these four contacts: what we do, how we look, what we say, and how we say it" (p. 159). Providing a way for students to practice, review, self-assess, and hone those skills will help prepare them for more effective communication in their future endeavors. Speaking is one of the Common Core State Standards' English language arts competencies (National Governors Association Center for Best Practices [NGA] & Council of Chief State School Officers [CCSSO], 2010), and communication is a crucial 21st century skill and one of P21's four Cs (Borowski, 2019). Any vision for cultivating 21st century skills requires embracing those tools and technologies.

Because communication is only effective if it works two ways, it is important to add a component to assessment that focuses on the receiving, or listening, side of communication. Listening, too, is one of the Common Core State Standards (NGA & CCSSO, 2010). Arming students with springboard questions will help them begin implementing these skills in daily communication. For example, having students search for the central idea and paraphrase it can increase close listening habits. Whether students are watching videos to learn from others or to critique themselves, providing prompts that focus on communication will produce results.

### Bolster Remote Teaching and Learning

The COVID-19 pandemic impacted every level of education across the globe, and education has permanently changed because of it. The question is, Do we try to force ourselves back into an outdated mold, or do we embrace some of the positive changes that are a result of the creativity and collaboration of the challenge?

Although some forms of virtual, distance, or remote learning have existed for some time, the pandemic brought these methods up for closer examination. Inevitably, many schools will adapt to the changing demands and continue to offer some form of remote learning. In fact, one study reports that:

> *Twenty percent of district and charter management organizations said . . . that they had started or were planning a virtual school or fully remote option this academic year and expected those options would remain after the pandemic. Another 10 percent said the same about hybrid or blended learning, while 7 percent said some lesser version of remote learning will continue when the pandemic is in the rearview mirror. (Superville, 2020)*

Building a video archive will propel teaching into the 21st century. For all the reasons videos make traditional classroom learning better, they work for and improve online learning as well (Vierstra, n.d.).

## Benefits for Teachers

Whether you are a new teacher or a seasoned professional, a video archive will positively impact your work. The COVID-19 pandemic may have pushed some educators into the digital realm, but many had already embraced using video to deliver content and will continue doing so regardless of circumstance. From art teachers to special education teachers, kindergarten through college prep, the various types of content recordings simply make teaching easier.

Just as student absences are unavoidable, so are teacher absences. Unfortunately, many teachers would argue that it is often more difficult to prepare for a substitute than it is worth. They would rather suffer through the illness and teach in person or pass up the opportunity to attend a professional development conference. In a survey of science teachers regarding attending professional development, one study finds that:

> *Lack of time and the schedule or timing of the professional development was an obstacle for a quarter of them. In addition, one-third of the first-year teachers said they were just trying to get through the year and felt there was no way they could or would take on anything else. (Fields, Levy, Karelitz, Martinez-Gudapakkam, & Jablonski, 2012, p. 45)*

If they have a video archive, teachers don't have to choose between teaching their class or taking care of themselves (either personally or professionally). Once you establish a video archive, taking time to attend conferences or to see a doctor becomes far less inconvenient and disruptive to students, staff, and you. If it is a planned absence, leaving directions for an alternative you is easier than writing a substitute plan. If you send lesson plans in an email or print them on a piece of paper, you can leave a website address for the day's lesson. The substitute simply plays your prerecorded lessons. For older students who follow a class calendar, it may be as simple as leaving directions for them to *Follow the link on the calendar for today*. If they have their own devices, they may be working independently during the class period, watching a recorded lesson while wearing headphones.

Educators have to consider their own health and safety as well as that of their students. This holds true whether the case is illness or a weather emergency. If students are able to access the videos, the class will go on. So, instead of worrying about how you will adjust your content in the event of a snow day, go ahead and sleep with those pajamas inside out and be sure to tuck a spoon under your pillow. (For those who have no need for snow shovels, blowers, and salt in the winter, these are folklore practices regarding ways to inspire snow days!)

The following are some of the key benefits for teachers in creating a video archive.

- Improve instruction based on self- and peer evaluation
- Provide students with increased equity
- Improve observation ability
- Save time
- Share easily with students and colleagues
- Provide insider perspective on student viewing habits

### *Improve Instruction Based on Self- and Peer Evaluation*

While earning National Board Certification, I was required to submit sample video lessons of my teaching as one element of demonstrating skill mastery. One possibly unintended consequence of the task was that I spent time really analyzing my teaching and classroom environment. I focused on what my students were doing in the videos, and this, in turn, made me think about how I was teaching.

This phenomenon is not unique to me. As it turns out, for over twenty years, researchers Miriam Gamoran Sherin and Elizabeth B. Dyer (2017) have been studying the effects of teachers using video to improve their instruction. They find that "video provides space for teachers to consider the intricacies of student thinking in ways that are not always possible during the moment of instruction" (Sherin & Dyer, 2017).

### *Provide Students With Increased Equity*

*Equity* means making sure all students have the resources and support they need to succeed (Kampen, 2020). Neurodivergent students, as well as those with physical and mental disabilities, are often at a disadvantage in school classrooms, but videos can allow teachers to present material in ways that reach these students (Kampen, 2020). As explained in the Get More Equitable Access for Attention Deficit Hyperactivity Disorder and Autism section (page 8), videos can increase equity by appealing to different sensory needs. Videos also increase equity because of their asynchronous access, which means students can view them at a time that better suits them.

Though I am not a special education teacher, many students in my classes have special needs. In some cases, an aid attends with them, but most times they navigate the course without one. One student, who had Tourette syndrome, was a highly functioning, intelligent senior who had managed his disability impressively for many years. He shared with me that public speaking class was the one he dreaded the most. He was self-conscious, hypercritical of himself, and nervous about having tics during other students' speeches and his own. His IEP allowed him to leave the classroom at any time he felt he could not control his tics. There were many days he felt he had to leave. Having a video archive for him to view allowed him to manage his disability and not lose connection with the class.

> Recorded lessons [for special needs students] make it easier to differentiate instruction that can be accessed at flexible times.
>
> **—Sarah Culbertson, elementary school special education teacher**
>
> I have students who are medically complex and often can't come to school due to lack of private-duty nurses to accompany them. [Videos give] my students at home an opportunity to continue to be a member of our classroom community and to continue to receive services. Students who in the past wouldn't be able to access instruction are now able to either join live remotely via video stream or watch recorded lessons of me doing actual instruction. It has opened up a huge opportunity for them!
>
> **—Angela McGuire, secondary special education teacher**

**TEACHER**
**VOICES**

### *Improve Observation Ability*

I will confess that for many years, I considered showing a video of myself reading a chapter to a class while I am *in* the class rather than reading the chapter in real time for the hundredth time. I always felt a little guilty about the idea. Somehow, it seemed wrong to show recordings if I were actually in the room, perfectly capable of reading the chapter again. What I hadn't considered is that video meets my digital native students where they are. One poll shows 90 percent of students explaining that they think video plays a critical role in the classroom (Kaltura, 2018). Students watch videos on their own all the time, and most are comfortable with that medium. Teachers are getting more comfortable with it, too. The same poll revealed that 97 percent of teachers regularly use video in the classroom, with just over half having students view videos as out-of-class work (Kaltura, 2018). While this research likely pertains to videos of content created by someone else, why not show videos of you, too?

I was struggling through bronchitis the first time I played a recording of myself reading instead of reading live. What a discovery! I was free to observe students' habits as they read along. Some were actively engaged, turning the pages at the correct time. Others were diligently completing the study guide questions as they read. A silent walk-through around the room provided a new lens. Most students engaged in reading, but one student looked like he had pulled an all-nighter. His forehead was on his desk, positioned to see the text in his lap. If I had been focusing on reading, I would not have noticed. Instead, I tapped his shoulder to get his attention. A quick email later in the day explaining my concern for him to his parents resulted in him redirecting his focus even more. Like many teens, he was not managing his screen time appropriately at bedtime.

Nonverbal cues to specific students—a quick point to the book, a nod of encouragement, a smile—are easy to do when you are not bound to delivering the content material. This immediate feedback may be crucial to student learning. One study revealed that feedback's timing can actually affect student retention (Opitz, Ferdinand, & Mecklinger, 2011). Just a delay of one second on feedback receipt affected cognition, and "the gain in performance was significantly larger for the group receiving immediate feedback as compared to the group receiving delayed feedback" (Opitz et al., 2011). Occasionally using video recordings of your own reading or instruction during class opens possibilities to your providing meaningful, timely feedback.

## Save Time

Sequential assignments that allow students to work at their own pace are terrific in theory, but they sometimes can be difficult to manage. Students reach various checkpoints at different times, often on different days, so whole-class instruction for various steps can become problematic. Some students may be ready for the next step, while those who are not ready may need a reiteration or deeper exploration of prior instruction. This means the teacher is continually cycling through steps.

Having a video archive of short tutorials—videos that the teacher records that give brief directions for a specific step of an assignment—saves time and energy. For example, in a research unit, a student who is still at the stage of searching for sources may not yet be ready to process information on how to format a works cited page. A short video with those directions will keep the student moving in the right direction when ready for that guidance. For example, if you teach a unit with sequential steps, you can create a Google Doc with the names of each step written in sequence and a hyperlink to directions. Using a single landing page for your class (I use the week-at-a-glance Google slideshow) will help make sure your students always know where to look. If you teach a unit spanning several days or weeks, you can add a link to a slideshow labeled Essential Links and include links to all the unit's resources there.

To a casual observer, the classroom experience may look very traditional. The teacher leads students through a lesson and models how to complete a step, followed by students trying it on their own. Videos are the difference—the underlying support. If students need reinforcement, you can direct students to the correct video based on what questions they ask. This saves time in the long run, freeing the teacher to respond to specific questions and issues that are not covered in the general tutorial videos.

## *Share Easily With Colleagues*

You can share a video archive not only with students, but also with colleagues. Whatever your school's video-hosting or virtual platform is, adding a like-subject colleague—even across grade levels—to your site instantly means sharing a wealth of knowledge and resources. Your school likely has a learning management system (LMS) for grades, attendance, and other student information, and where students can locate classroom and other resources. In Canvas, for example, you can add a co-teacher to your course, granting full access to a colleague to all of your course resources. However, you don't need a school-sanctioned LMS to share content. You can use free services such as Google, YouTube, and Vimeo to upload content, set your privacy settings, and share.

This kind of sharing among teachers is directly related to the kind of collaboration that has positive effects on student achievement (Mora-Ruano, Heine, & Gebhardt, 2019), as they "enhance teacher effectiveness and expertise" (Hattie, 2015, as cited in Mora-Ruano et al., 2019). Beginning teachers will benefit by watching lessons taught by a more experienced teacher before covering the material in class. Similarly, student teachers can observe a vast number of classes in preparation for taking the lead in the classroom. Special education teachers can tap into the video archive to support their students. For example, if they have full access to a teacher's course, they can preview, review, and reinforce lessons on video with students during a guided study period.

In 2013, my own school district launched a professional development opportunity in which all teachers were required to select a colleague and observe that colleague teaching a specified number of times per year. This initiative was one that teachers welcomed because it gave them insights into other teaching styles, techniques, and methods across the curriculum. The problem became logistics. This plan only worked if a teacher wanted to observe a colleague who did not have a common prep period. The stars needed to align for both the observer and the observed to coordinate a period that was convenient and meaningful. In contrast, sharing your archive with colleagues eliminates the logistical barriers of time conflict.

Colleagues can observe as many lessons as they choose, whenever and however they choose, causing absolutely no extra work for or disruption to the observed teacher. The observing teacher needn't miss teaching his or her class, either.

This seamless sort of sharing that traditionally takes coordination, time, and facilitation also benefits the observed teacher, who can more readily seek feedback from observers. Coaches can watch a recorded lesson at their own convenience with an eye for specific growth opportunities. Education experts Emily Dolci Grimm, Trent Kaufman, and Dave Doty (2014) explore the benefits of observation: Teachers are bound by their own schedules and demands. They do not have the flexibility to observe whatever and whenever they want. Using video removes these restrictions because the observer can view the videos when convenient. The teacher who is to be observed can record when convenient. A teacher can learn and improve by watching the process. Sharing an insider glimpse into the workings of a classroom with a video archive will guide others on their own successful path to teaching.

Seasoned and newer teachers alike can find themselves restless with stale material and worn-out methods. Watching another teacher approach the same—or a different—subject can help teachers improve their own practice. Lessons that were stuck in a rut can come back to life when a teacher has an opportunity to see them from a new perspective.

## Provide Insider Perspective on Student Viewing Habits

Requiring students to independently engage in content and practice skills and monitor them as they do so are educational best practices (Rosenshine, 2012). Depending on what platform you or your district uses, you may be able to track which students have viewed a video. Some platforms will provide specific details about exactly how much of the video the student watched. If you find that students are not tapping into your video resources, try to figure out why. Maybe they feel that they have a solid grasp on the material and do not believe they need them. If the videos are intended to be supplemental, then that is fine. For students who stumble along the way—due to illness, absences, or some other roadblock—it is essential that all know how to find the videos should they ever need them. Other students may not realize or remember that the archive exists, or perhaps they just don't know how to access it. This is why simple organization is key.

Check regularly to see if students know how to access videos. Provide a link to your video-hosting website on the whiteboard and on your LMS, and consider providing a QR code. (There are free generators, such as QR Code Generator at www.qr-code-generator.com, online.) For elementary and middle school students, provide parents and guardians a physical copy of instructions with the URL. If you send the instructions via email, include a direct link to your video-hosting website.

## About This Book

Once you have decided to embark on recording yourself teaching, the book will lead you through how to get started, including skill development, accessing technology, and classroom logistics, as well as how to engage your students in the recording and accessing process. I will walk you through the steps of building a video archive. Along the way, you will find helpful resources such as reproducibles to use in your classroom and tips and testimonials to encourage you every step of the way. Your archive will grow as you go, and I will help you recognize recording opportunities that capture your practice for future reference.

- Chapter 1 explores the various types of videos you may create and their benefits, including but not limited to whole-class discussion, enhancement tutorials, and enrichment lessons.

- Chapter 2 helps you get started for the school year, with a to-do checklist of video setup and communication considerations, as well as considerations for future archives.

- Chapter 3 helps you build confidence in yourself and in your students so that speaking in front of a video camera works better for everyone.

Chapters will include the following.

- Reproducibles for use in your own practice
- Try This for practical tasks that will help you establish your video archive
- Teacher Tips to improve the process, save you time, and improve student learning and outcomes
- Pandemic Perspective insights for the teacher who wants to learn and grow from the COVID-19 lessons
- Student Voices and Teacher Voices from the 2020–2021 school year to provide insight, directly from students and teachers who have used videos, about the advantages they have experienced

Keep your smartphone handy while you read. You will need it when you see the QR codes that appear throughout the book. The codes link to videos that pertain to the surrounding text, and there are endnotes showing the URLs themselves at the end of each chapter. Follow these steps to read the QR code and see the video.

1. Open your smartphone camera.

2. Aim your phone's camera at the QR code (but don't actually photograph it). The camera will show tiny yellow brackets around the corner of the square and a pop-up will prompt you to "Open in YouTube [or Google, or similar]."

3. Tap the prompt to go directly to the video.

New initiatives can feel overwhelming. Most teachers can relate to the good idea overload that goes along with the back-to-school in-service days in the fall. Creating videos and archiving does not mean a plunge into the icy depths of the new initiatives ocean. Take it as slowly as you need to, getting comfortable at a pace that suits you. Dip your toes or dive deep. There are a plethora of benefits for students—access during absences, personalized review speed, assessment preparation, and virtual learning. Teachers benefit too, through easy sharing and collaboration, and—a rare gift for teachers— by saving time. You might only want to dabble but then start to see real benefits and decide to go further. You might even begin having fun with it. Do as little or as much as suits your needs.

*Chapter 1*

# Creating a Diverse Archive Throughout the School Year

Let's face it, educators know better than most that new initiatives come and go quickly. Each year, districts around the country are recognized as the pioneers of innovative initiatives that give their students the cutting edge. Every fall there seems to be a new focus or agenda guiding teachers to revolutionize the industry to serve students better. Some stand the test of time, but many do not.

The concept of building a video archive is not just a new fad or acronym that an obscure administrator from the district office will present in the fall, never to be seen or heard from again. This is a personal approach to making your classroom better. Period. It will be better for you, better for your students, and better for everyone who wants to help students learn (families, administrators, support teachers, and others). Best of all, every ounce of effort that you put into creating classroom videos will continue to pay you back year after year. As long as you maintain your archive, you will always have the work that you are doing right now for future use. Maintenance will require you to develop a system of organization so that you can easily find and share videos. Every classroom has its own culture and dynamics, with some heavily focused on teacher-led content and others leaning more toward student-driven discussions and group projects. Whatever the typical day looks like in your classroom, there is a way to capture its essence and make it more accessible to everyone who will benefit.

Once you develop the mindset of seeking opportunities to record, you will be amazed by how many different types of recordings you can create to make both your teaching and your students' learning more effective.

This chapter explores the following videos for a classroom archive.

- Recording different types of videos
- Recording specific subjects and approaches
- Using video for professional growth

Creating a diverse video archive will enhance your teaching and free you to take care of other pressing duties that strain your time. Plan to record a variety of types of videos for multiple purposes.

## Recording Different Types of Videos

Every class is unique. Countless variables—from the individual students, to the time of day that class takes place, to the course content itself—constitute your classroom's culture. While this is true, the essence of your instruction will likely fall into a few distinct categories—a lecture, small-group time, or interactive teacher-led discussion, for example. Whatever the case, there is a rationale for recording each type of lesson. Regardless of what you are recording, consider the guidelines in figure 1.1.

---

Keep these guidelines in mind as you record.

- Hold phones horizontally.
- Brace yourself against something solid if you're handholding. Don't hold the phone or camera in midair.
- Direct the camera at whoever is speaking (not necessarily at the teacher).
- Break at frequent, logical points, such as the end of a chapter or when transitioning to a new subject. (There is no need to record physical movements such as moving desks or passing out papers. At the secondary level, consider recording a full period, and then recording shorter segments in a different period of the same subject later the same day, so you can share the full class for an absent student but have smaller segments to share for review or future classes.)
- *Pan*, or swivel the camera in a horizontal movement, slowly. Don't make quick movements.
- Upload the video in a timely manner (such as before leaving each day, so absent students can watch them for the next day).

---

Figure 1.1: Recording guidelines.

*Visit **go.SolutionTree.com/technology** for a free reproducible version of this figure.*

If you teach a class more than once in a day (as many secondary teachers do), try recording more than one class delivery of the same content. Select the one that went the smoothest for the video archive. Fortunately, one of my classes is on an alternating-day schedule, so I have twenty-four hours before repeating the lesson each time. This *marinating* time lets me think about how things might have gone better. The next day I have another chance to improve the delivery and usually end up archiving the recording of the B-day class instead.

When students ask questions about material covered in a tutorial video, it is often a sign that the student did not watch the video. Follow up and ask if he or she watched the video. Sometimes this is a wake-up call for students to take advantage of the video archive for learning in the class (both in the classroom and at home). Tutorials are an excellent way to reinforce concepts.

**TEACHER TIP**

## *Whole-Class Discussion*

One of the easiest types of videos to record is a whole-class discussion because the camera can remain stationary. When you position the camera for whole-class discussions, "make sure you're capturing ALL [sic] of the presenting space" (GoReact, n.d., p. 3). If all desks face the front of the room, position the camera on a tripod in the back of the room. If you prefer to focus more on student responses, you may want to position the camera in the front of the classroom facing students. (Be sure to secure permission before recording students. See page 54.) Whichever you decide, do a sound check. *External microphones* (those not built into your phone or video recorder) work best (GoReact, n.d.). I have had success with my smartphone, but the more classroom noise there is, the more difficult it is to capture good sound. You may want to consider investing in microphones that connect to the computer that can be placed around the room.

The desks in my room are split in half down two sides of the room, with short rows of three or four facing the other side of the room, like you see in figure 1.2 (page 26). I sit on a stool at the far end of the classroom between the facing rows. This way I have easy eye contact with the full class. I position the camera on the opposite side of the classroom from me and record in a wide, horizontal angle to easily capture the full class.

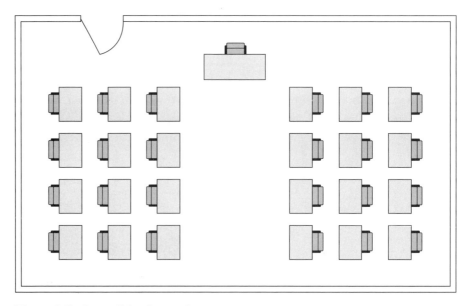

**Figure 1.2: A possible class setup.**

Consider a modified Four Corners activity, described in the following steps, as a different kind of example. As long as you have a student willing to operate the camera (or have it set to record on a tripod), you can easily capture organic discussions that will be helpful for absent students or for those who want to access the video for review. If you choose to record the small-group discussions in the corners, you may want to record yourself when you visit each group. Otherwise, you may choose to record only the whole-class discussion after the small groups have had time to discuss. Recording the speaker for each group will allow students to consider the depth of the opposing choices more deeply.

Follow these steps to do the modified Four Corners activity.

1. Create signs—Agree, Somewhat Agree, Somewhat Disagree, and Disagree—and post them in four separate spots in your room (though not too far from each other, for ease of recording).

2. Begin recording and introduce the topic for debate by having students provide a synopsis of pro and con research articles representing multiple viewpoints. Depending on the age group, this may have been assigned reading for homework prior to the activity, or it may be an in-class reading prior to the discussion.

3. After students present the synopsis, read a statement pertaining to the topic about which students must literally take a position in the classroom by moving to the area with the sign that corresponds to their opinion.

4.  It is optional, but not necessary, to record this small-group discussion time. Allow sufficient time for the students to discuss their position with those who are like-minded in their corner of the room. Ask each group to designate a spokesperson to summarize the group's rationale for taking this position.

5.  Begin recording again (if you have stopped) and rotate around the room to allow the spokesperson for each of the four corners to make a statement.

6.  Allow students to change their positions, literally walking to join another group, based on each group's statement.

7.  Encourage students to take notes to capture key points that peers make throughout the debate. See figure 1.3 for a form they can use. At this point, you may have a whole-class discussion, allowing someone from one group to respond to comments from another.

8.  Assign this task to students: using the recording of the articles' synopsis, the pros and cons, as well as each group's statement and the whole-class discussion, write a persuasive essay to support your position on the topic and refute the opposing arguments. Make citation a requirement (a specific number of direct or paraphrased quotes from the discussion and a specific number of citations from the articles) to maximize the potential for students to engage in both the live debate and the recording.

Whatever activity you choose to implement to generate a whole-class discussion, try to capture anything that is beneficial to hear again. Imagine

| Complete the notes for each position. Be sure to note each spokesperson's name for reference in paper. | |
| --- | --- |
| Agree spokesperson: | Somewhat Agree spokesperson: |
| Disagree spokesperson: | Somewhat Disagree spokesperson: |

Figure 1.3: Debate note form.

*Visit* **go.SolutionTree.com/technology** *for a free reproducible version of this figure.*

yourself as an absent student from your class. What would be essential to capture to ensure that you were able to follow and understand the missed content? That's what you record!

---

**STUDENT**
**VOICES**

I think [videos are] better than Zoom meetings because in Zoom or other virtual hangouts, people don't want to raise their hands and ask questions. Those videos show kids asking questions—a lot of them which I have—and it lends itself well to getting my questions answered.

**—Eleventh-grade student**

---

**TEACHER**
**VOICES**

A live classroom video recording captures a more authentic recorded lesson that includes student responses and anecdotes that may not have occurred with a prerecorded video or lesson.

**—TJ Reuteman, high school mathematics teacher**

I created and edited together about thirty videos last year. I am getting near to the point in my curriculum where I can start reusing some of those videos. This will help since I am now in full virtual mode. The videos are not a perfect substitute for the in-class experience, but it will give me some time to plan other aspects of my virtual lessons.

**—John Harder, high school science teacher**

---

## Assignment Instructions

I distinctly remember the cycle of embarrassing self-doubt and paranoia in a specific high school class I took in which the teacher made it clear that if someone asked a question that she had already answered in class, they were obviously not listening. The message for me was loud and clear: don't ask questions! I always assumed that my question was one that the teacher had probably already covered, and I did not want to be the one humiliated in front of the class. I went to great lengths to avoid speaking to the teacher at all costs, consulting my peers first if I needed help. Particularly when this teacher sent us to the library, we were set loose to do research on our own to demonstrate our own ability to navigate the vast information available to us.

While I believe that educators have made great strides in the areas of communication and student self-advocacy, this feeling of lingering doubt is alive and well in students everywhere, especially in a subject area that may be out of a student's comfort zone. The library may be just one example where many students feel out of place and plagued by self-doubt. In fact, a study that surveyed college students' feelings about using the library found that "(1) students generally feel that their own library-use skills are inadequate while the skills of other students are adequate, (2) the inadequacy is shameful and should be hidden, and (3) the inadequacy would be revealed by asking questions" (Mellon, 2015). If college students feel inadequate and ashamed, how must younger students feel? If they are intimidated (intentionally or not) by the teachers and librarians, how much learning is *not* happening as a result?

How do we break this cycle of self-doubt and apprehension in asking questions? One simple solution is to create an overview video that introduces an assignment and walks students through the steps. Another type is the tutorial for instructions that students can access at will when they get stuck—or when they want to work ahead! If you find yourself repeating something more than twice, whether it is assignment directions or an explanation of material, it is worth your while to make a quick recording of it. Especially with technical directions, directing your students to a specific spot on a video rather than taking the time to repeat the directions again will become second nature.

Before you begin, prepare by writing a plan and ensuring the environment is well lit and quiet (Creative Bloq, 2013). While it is possible to edit video, with a short tutorial, it is more likely that you will just rerecord if someone interrupts or you really lose your train of thought. Don't forget to turn your phone to airplane mode to avoid disruptions. The QR codes on this page lead to brief videos of assignment instructions.

**Debate instruction[1]**

**Thesis statement instruction[2]**

Recording demonstrations for hands-on projects is crucial regardless of the current teaching or learning model or environment.

—Samantha Smith, high school art teacher

**TEACHER VOICES**

**PANDEMIC**
**PERSPECTIVE**

Many of my students shared in their daily journals that they were struggling to establish a routine and keeping terrible sleep schedules. Without a rigid start time to their days, students were struggling to manage their schoolwork, sleep, and online fun time. They were binge watching seasons of their favorite shows until the early hours of the morning and sleeping through daily optional office hours. Although a more disciplined approach to managing their lives would have been ideal, I needed to find a way to teach to my audience—teenagers who didn't live by the alarm clock. Creating tutorials allowed me to post relevant information for the day that they could access at 2:00 a.m. if necessary. For elementary students, these tutorials would be helpful for parents who may need to help their children (or who are working during the day during virtual learning). Tapping into tutorials in the evening hours to help students with homework can clear up a great deal of confusion. When I think back to the many homework assignments that I tried to help my own children navigate when they were young, I believe that tutorials would have been very helpful!

## Enhancement Tutorials

One of the most helpful discoveries I have made in developing my archive is the value of short enhancement tutorial videos. These are short videos—typically no more than five minutes long—that provide more details about the bigger topic I am presenting in class. For example, if I am clarifying a text's historical context, I may have an enhancement video that goes more in depth on a specific historical detail that would enrich students' knowledge but is not essential to studying the work as a whole. I think of them as embedded hyperlinks in my teaching style.

Creating tutorials that are full of helpful information but not so long that students will lose interest is a challenge. Exploring classroom strategies by sixth-grade mathematics teacher Andrea Smith, Bill Tucker (2011), managing director of Education Sector, explains:

> Crafting a great four- to six-minute video lesson poses a tremendous instructional challenge: how to explain a concept in a clear, concise, bite-sized chunk. Creating her own videos forces her to

*pay attention to the details and nuances of instruction—the pace, the examples used, the visual representation, and the development of aligned assessment practices.*

**Enhancement tutorial[3]**

When I share a video with my class, my time expands to a new dimension. For example, when I introduce a unit on William Golding's (1954/2011) *Lord of the Flies*, I have a slide presentation that walks the class through the historical context of World War II, when the novel is set, and the literary elements of allegory and themes. I am not, by any means, advocating replacing the classroom teacher with videos. Enhancement videos are intended to do just that: *enhance*. They serve a very specific purpose—to improve learning (if time permits, if students desire a deeper dig into the material, and so on). The presentation takes about thirty minutes. Depending on the actual time I have for a specific class, I may present the basic version (without showing the videos on the embedded hyperlinks to the class); however, the embedded video elements are available for the students to pursue outside of the class period to enhance their learning further. If I have wiggle room to show a video to further information, I will. If not, the presentation is stored in the class platform, and students can access the videos via the links on their own time. The first QR code on this page takes you to an enhancement tutorial about wartime rationing in Britain.

**Physics enrichment[4]**

The presentation page in figure 1.4 (page 32) shows the notes included in a presentation that remind the teacher and cue the students about which slides have additional information embedded. Whether I create the enhancement video myself or find an exemplar online, the opportunity for enriched learning is there for students who want or need more learning outside the rigid confines of the class period. Although you may not choose to show every enhancement video during class, when it comes time to prepare for an assessment, students may find the enhancement videos helpful.

Be creative with your enhancement videos. For example, in this unit that I teach, I may have videos that are literature related (literary terms explored in depth), history related (newsreel footage of WWII rationing), movie clips (cinematic illustrations of evacuations for air-raid drills), or author and film adaptation related (an interview with the author about writing the book, or with the movie director about making the film). Taking a similar approach for another subject area, a physics teacher may have enhancement videos of biographical information about a particular physicist, examples of modern technology built on the principles of the physicist's work, an example of how to test a theory, or cutting-edge theories. A classroom lesson is restricted by the physical time and space of the classroom, but enhancement videos are limitless. The second QR code on this page links to a video about a physics discovery for enrichment.

### Allegory

- **Allegory:** a way of explaining things which cannot easily be explained by telling a story which has a deeper but related meaning.
- An allegory is a form of extended metaphor, in which objects, persons, and actions in a narrative are equated with the meanings that lie outside the narrative itself.
- The underlying meaning has moral, social, religious, or political significance, and characters are often personifications of abstract ideas such as charity, greed, or envy. Thus, an allegory is a story with two meanings, a literal meaning and symbolic meaning.
- It is important to understand the context of an allegory if you want to understand the meaning beyond the literal level.

Hyperlink to sixty-second video clip of a definition of allegory on the slide title.

Figure 1.4: Example presentation page.

I use a free version of Screencastify (www.screencastify.com) that limits recordings to five minutes. If I can't manage my material in five minutes, I need to tweak it and try again. This requires me to really focus and not waste any time with filler words or tangents. One way to do this is to simply practice. Generally, after practicing once or twice, I will settle on a purposeful pace. Another trick is to write a bulleted list of main points you want to make in a place that you can easily see, or place sticky notes with key words around the computer monitor before you record.

**TEACHER VOICES**

I record myself teaching math games or teaching a skill, and then I ask for students to watch them during their in-class independent work time. This saves me time to lead more strategy groups.

—Heidi Byer, fourth-grade teacher

### *Teacher-Led Close Text Reading*

Record teacher-led close text reading with *only* you to avoid the need for securing permission to use the video. The teacher's guiding questions will guide viewers, as well, and the students do not need to appear in the video. Much like how commercials for toys or other physical products are often shot showing just the hands of someone playing or using it, these videos allow the reader to "play along" with the teacher's guidance, putting him or herself in the position of the participant.

As different initiatives have come and gone throughout the decades, literacy and improved reading comprehension are important at every level of instruction or subject. Guided reading has many variations, but the commonality among all is that the teacher is involved in leading students, either independently or in groups, through reading text. Regie Routman (2018b), author of the book *Literacy Essentials: Engagement, Excellence, and Equity for All Learners* (Routman, 2018a), claims, "Guided reading is and always has been a means to an end—readers who love to read for pleasure, information, enrichment, life fulfillment, and their own personal goals." This often involves scaffolding, such as providing context before reading, pausing for clarification and questions throughout the reading, and discussing the text. Whatever subject matter or grade level you teach, reading is essential for learning. Leading students in guided reading has value in the classroom, including beyond elementary school, where such guided reading is common. Literacy expert Timothy Shanahan (2018) advises something uncommon:

> At secondary level, I would certainly include various kinds of communal reading—under teacher guidance . . . whether we are talking about the reading of a short story in an English class or a chapter from a science book. Such communal reading opportunities well managed promote mature interpretations of particular texts or the development of comprehension strategies.

Taking the time in class to lead guided reading will affect students' literacy levels, but having a video of the lesson available for students to review on their own or with a support person has the potential to increase learning exponentially. Add the built-in benefit of adjusting the speed of the video to slow down or speed up depending on listener comfort levels, and the impact is remarkable. Then layer the impact of using this guided reading recording for future use, and the learning potential and value of the recording grows even further. Across the curriculum, in mathematics class, a teacher may guide students through a specific type of word problem, providing scaffolding by asking questions to guide the student. In a world language class, a teacher may lead a small group through text written in a foreign language, prompting with context clues and questions to help students decipher meaning.

**STUDENT VOICES**

Leaving early for a golf match or a baseball game was a common occurrence, and since English 10 was my last class of the day, I missed it often. Generally, the days that I missed were spent reading and analyzing books such as *Lord of the Flies* (Golding, 1954/2011) and *A Tale of Two Cities* (Dickens, 1859/2007). As a student, reading these challenging books alone is very difficult and something that I had struggled with in the past. However, in English 10, I was able to follow along with videos of former classes analyzing the text that not only helped me keep up with my work, but excel in my learning. These videos not only helped me catch up after I missed class but allowed me to work ahead when I knew I was going to miss class. I was even able to use the videos to go back and reread parts of the book that I didn't understand.

—**Eleventh-grade student**

**Chapter reading[5]**

I have read Golding's (1954/2011) *Lord of the Flies* aloud to students at least thirty-forty times, and every time I do, I discover something new. Whether a student asks an insightful question in discussion or my mind takes an uncharted path, the discovery affects the way that I interpret the text the next time I read it. The point is that my own comprehension and ownership of the text are fluid; therefore, my videos should be as well. I may choose to alter my inflection based on the discovery to emphasize a phrase, draw attention to ominous wording by slowing my delivery, or pause for dramatic effect. Every time I make a change is an opportunity to improve my video recording of the reading to replace in the archive. This holds true for class readings, discussions, and lecture deliveries. If something is better (as it usually will be!) the second (or fortieth) time, then take advantage of the improvement by recording it. The QR code on this page leads to a video of me reading a chapter from the book.

## Review Sessions

It took me until my college days before I realized that I needed to sit as close to the professor as I possibly could to do well. Hairstyles, shoes, backpacks, someone's doodles on his or her notes—they all distracted me. Most students struggle with distractions of some sort, and many do not take action to fix the situation because they either don't realize it or simply prefer to be socially rather than academically focused. Even the best students can fall victim to the drama happening all around them. If students struggle to focus within the physical space and time of your class period, providing a video for them to review in a less distracting environment could help them improve their performance on assessments.

**Whole-class review session[6]**

One of the biggest challenges for students who struggle with tests and assessments is simply not knowing how to best prepare. There is often a disconnect at home when a parent asks, "Did you study?" and the student believes that he or she did. Some students do not know how to prepare for assessments and use a one-size-fits-all approach to studying. Knowing the format, type, and style of an assessment makes a big difference in preparing. For example, a test on anatomical body parts and functions requires a different skill set than an open-note literary analysis. At the elementary level, prepping for a timed mathematics test looks very different from memorizing the states and their capitals. If your class includes a specific style of assessment, consider sharing a recording of a review session from a unit that a previous class did *before* you begin the unit with the new group of students.

How you record a review video will depend on the type of assessment you will conduct in class. Interactive review games, like a Jeopardy! board, engage the full class, so you will decide if you want the full class in view or just a screencast of the game board. The advantage of a screencast is that no students will be visible in the recording, so permissions are not an issue. In history classes, for a focused essay, you may want to record a chalk talk of students planning a response for a sample prompt on a SMART Board. This could also be a screencast in which you record only the SMART Board while students brainstorm.

Keep in mind that review recordings can be very helpful to future classes, so if permission to record students is an issue, screen recording with voices only may be the best option. One type of recording that completely sidesteps the issue of student images and permission is the teacher review tutorial. A screen recording of you presenting a Google slideshow with a webcam recording image in the corner allows you to share tips and strategies directly with students and their support networks. Students can watch as many times as necessary, pause, reflect, plan, and prepare. The QR code on this page takes you to a review session.

Having an idea of the end goal in mind from the beginning will help students prepare in meaningful ways and guide them to focus on the concepts and aspects of learning that they will need to master to do well. For example, if vocabulary is on a unit test, seeing a video of students playing a review game that requires them to both know definitions and correctly use words in context will cue students watching the video to prepare in this manner, especially if they are watching a sample review just to get a better feel for the class. Of course, teachers should clearly communicate course objectives and summative assessment details from the start of any unit, but sometimes seeing the review in action will resonate more with students than the spoken directions. Students will cultivate effective study skills from the start of the unit rather than trying to cram information.

**STUDENT**
**VOICES**

I used [the review videos] for writing notes on subjects I either missed or [wrote] confusing notes on.

**—Tenth-grade student**

The video provided better review than a study guide, because it was almost the same lesson we went over in class. Because of this, I was able to recall information better.

**—Tenth-grade student**

Often, when students show signs of confusion midway through a unit, I recommend that they go back to where they last understood what was happening and listen from that point in the book we are studying. I share that this is one of my own habits when listening to an audiobook or podcast. I just back up thirty seconds at a time until I find familiar footing. Often, I listen to the first chapter twice to ensure my understanding. It is always surprising to me when I catch something new on the second listen that changes my foundational understanding of the book. Students may discover that they misunderstood something early that affects their current understanding. Backing up can fix the issue and get them back on track. You may even be able to direct the students to a specific spot in a book or lecture to review if they are confused about a key concept or plot twist.

Admittedly, I was the butt of the joke among my friends and family for years as I was the English teacher who didn't have time to read any books. I always claimed that I was too busy reading students' papers to have any free time to read something of my own choosing for pleasure. This all radically changed with my discovery of audiobooks. I found myself listening to at least a book a week and even started a tradition of listening to favorites throughout the seasons. I flew through the classics and even stepped into the best sellers displayed on the shelves at the local bookstore—all while doing the activities I had always done: walking my dogs, folding laundry, cleaning the house. For an attendance question, I selected, What are you currently reading for fun? It was a disheartening day to say the least. My bright-eyed honors students looked dejected. They were not reading anything nor *had they* read anything by choice in ages. They thought they were too busy, or perhaps they just didn't like to read for fun.

Students can review problems and notes whenever they want, so questions in the classroom transform from *how* to complete a problem to *why* the certain problem-solving strategy is correct.

—John Wilkinson, high school physics teacher

**TEACHER**
VOICES

That is when I shared my secret. Listening to audiobooks is the key to squeezing pleasure reading back into one's life (or enjoying books for the first time). After sharing my discovery, many students gave it a try. They reported back to me within a few weeks about how much they were enjoying reading again. They hadn't realized how much time they had in their lives to listen, even if they didn't have time to sit and read. I challenged them with my own yearly reading quest: to listen to J. K. Rowling's (2009) Harry Potter series from start to finish, beginning on the first day of spring break. No matter what plans (or lack of plans) I have for spring break, I know that I am spending it with "friends" that I love. Once I shared my plan, I was surprised by how many students reported after spring break that they had taken my challenge and done the same thing.

Certainly, there are some texts students would benefit from reading in print; however, having an audio option is an added benefit. If students are absent on a day that we are reading a specific chapter of a book, they have access to me reading it on a video. The recordings are available on the classroom platform for them to listen on the go, if necessary: commuting to school, eating breakfast, and so on. They can adjust the recording's playback speed (going up to 1.25 or down to .75, for example) to suit their pace.

**PANDEMIC**
**PERSPECTIVE**

My students love to play review games, but I struggled during the early days of the pandemic to find an effective platform to hold a full-class review session in real time. Instead, I was able to share a video from my archive to help the students review for an assessment. Although I am sure that they would have preferred the real-life competition of the review, they did not miss the opportunity to learn. In fact, they had access to the review several days prior to the assessment the following week, so in some ways, they may have even had an advantage over the traditional in-class review method.

**Lecture[7]**

## Lectures

A face-to-face delivery of material allows for give and take. Students can pose questions. Teachers can gauge faces for understanding and improvise based on comprehension. The key element for recording a lecture is to capture everything in the presentation: teacher (including shoulders and hands to include gestures, if possible), display or whiteboard, and sound. Whether you are recording a live lecture in the classroom or creating a video through a program such as Screencastify in which you can record your screen with a webcam, capturing the material and your voice is the key to a good recording. The QR code on this page takes you to a typical lecture video.

Videos are not an equal substitute for human interaction, but they can certainly assist in teaching. I learned this in 2011 when my daughter suffered a severe concussion. She was too embarrassed to reveal this at the time, but she secretly recorded her AP history teacher's lectures by hiding her phone in her backpack during class. Months later, when we were on a long spring break road trip, I noticed her in the back seat mindlessly staring out the window with her headphones in. When I asked what she was doing, she said she was studying for AP exams. Sitting in class at the time of her concussion was nearly a waste of time. Her short-term recall was severely impaired, but thankfully she had the presence of mind to invest in her own future by recording the lectures. The benefit of having a recording of a teacher's lecture to review prior to an assessment can make a significant difference in a student's readiness to demonstrate understanding of the concepts.

When I was teaching at home virtually with children of my own, I was able to flip my classroom and video record at convenient times for me and plan asynchronous lessons for the whole group that freed up time for me to work synchronously with small groups and individuals who needed more support.

—**Kathleen Evans, high school English teacher**

**TEACHER**
**VOICES**

## *Student Presentations*

Students may record their presentations on a program such as Screencastify or Flipgrid and submit them for teacher (and maybe even peer) review. Another option is to record a live presentation in class of students. Distance learners can easily share their screens during their presentations, revealing both their webcam and their visual. I have had both remote and face-to-face students present in class. It takes a bit of coordination, but I do not underestimate how resourceful students can be. One student may be standing in front of the class presenting at the whiteboard while a partner follows along, jumping in to speak on cue for a joint presentation that the distance learner is screen sharing. In this manner, both students are visible to the class, and only one of them is physically present. The QR code on this page links to a video of a group presentation.

Group
presentation[8]

Whether it is a musical compilation, a history reenactment skit, an explain-your-work response, or a book report, student presentations are a key component to education. Recording individual and group presentations does the following.

- Creates a record of the project to review for assessment (and to refer to should there be any questions about grading)

- Allows students to share their products with their parents and guardians

- Enables their self-assessment (page 104)

- Functions as exemplars to share with future students working on a similar project (Be sure to secure permission.)

- Provides evidence of student mastery of concepts that you may review when writing letters of recommendation for students

- Serves as evidence of your teaching effectiveness in your teaching portfolio for your district review

## *Supplemental or Enrichment Lessons*

Sometimes we just run out of time. The basketball team makes it to state, so there is an impromptu all-school assembly that cuts into class time. New state requirements spring standardized testing on students for multiple days within a single term. The list of disruptions goes on and on. There is no need to feel that you are watering down the curriculum to fit the new time restrictions. If you have a video archive ready to go, you can assign supplemental material to accommodate the real-time schedule. For example, there have been times when my sophomores have morning testing for three days in a row. Having both morning and afternoon classes of sophomores makes this type of disruption the biggest challenge. It is difficult to keep classes in sync when one meets and the other does not. In my case, having a video archive for the morning sophomores to access as homework kept my classes on track with each other.

You may also find that having an extra unit up your sleeve can come in handy for all kinds of unusual circumstances. For example, I once had a student in my public speaking class who needed to travel across the country for medical treatments. He was not able to attend class physically during these times, so having an entire unit ready to roll out for him to complete on his own time made the situation work for him. It was not extra work for me because I had saved everything for convenient access in my video archive. All I needed to do was share it with him.

As teachers, we tend to advocate that learning is the goal and grades are secondary. Ask high school students who are shooting for an acceptance letter from a particular college and they would not agree. For them, grades matter. Giving students an opportunity to raise their grades—should they choose to take on an extra challenge of an enrichment unit—gives them greater autonomy. You may alternately or additionally allow retakes that allow students to learn from failure without negatively impacting their grades (Barack, 2019; Zeiser et al., 2018). Both of these options also provide the opportunity to demonstrate students' drive to discover as they take control of their educational experience. Adding assessments worth extra points to the overall points of a term can diffuse a unit that did not go as well as they would have liked. If you have an additional unit ready to launch, students can choose to do it or not based on their own motivational levels.

Generally, a supplemental unit is one that is ready to go and is interchangeable with one that you teach in the current curriculum. It covers the course objectives in the same way, but the material is different. For example, I may substitute a unit on a particular novel with reading a play, or exchange a written personal narrative writing piece with a TED Talk-style speech. As long as the unit addresses the course objectives, there is flexibility. An enrichment unit may be a special assignment that goes deeper into a unit of study—for example, a case study of a historical Supreme Court case in a U.S. history class that is examining the civil rights movement of the 1960s. This enrichment material adds scaffolding to the main unit, but it is not essential for learning the historical implications of the time period. Having enrichment units or assignments for students who show desire to learn more can provide the extra challenge that they need. There's no need to worry about extra work for yourself, either. Enrichment activities can culminate in student presentations that may take hours of preparation for the student, but minutes of time for you and the class to view.

Similarly, you can use supplemental units as substitute material for students. For example, for the last week of my term, I usually do a full-class unit of a Shakespeare play, but it is not a required element of the course. I give my students the option of doing a supplemental unit instead of the in-class reading of the play. They work independently in class on this project while the rest of the class engages in the play. While the optional unit is a direct substitute for what we are doing in class, I also offer the option to do both units. For students who enjoy the extra enrichment, or simply want the opportunity to boost their grades with an additional assessment, this gives them choice that may affect their overall grade. The key point here is that this creates very little additional work for me. Having the video archive ready to go keeps everyone happy.

As much as we may like to believe that each student who enters our classroom is a blank slate ready to learn and achieve, the reality is that each student walks into our world with a wealth of experiences. Inevitably, a new student tells me at least once a year, "I read this last year in my old school." While some students welcome the opportunity to float easily through a unit that they have already studied, enrichment is the way to go. Another scenario is when a student is repeating a course for grade improvement. Rather than guiding that student through the exact material for a second round, he or she may have more success with a fresh start on something new. You may find that there are times when the usual units that you teach feel like a poor match for the current environment. This is especially true when teaching literature if subject matter covers particularly sensitive topics. For example, the unfortunate reality is that many schools have grieved the loss of a student. It may feel too raw to read a piece of literature that focuses on the topic of death in the immediate days or weeks following the loss. There are other works of literature to choose that will meet course objectives in a more sensitive way for that term. In health class, the teacher may rotate curriculum to deal with mental health awareness in the wake of a student death. On a positive note, an economics teacher might do a close study of the stock market response to a rise in cryptocurrency if it is making headlines. Adapting to the current climate by having alternate units in the bullpen is a way to keep things fresh for students and yourself.

If the course objectives and learning targets are broad, you may find it helpful to have alternative units to substitute for the term. You don't need an alternate unit for every unit in your course. Seasoned teachers generally have units waiting in the wings, but new teachers can benefit from others' experiences. Sharing units and materials is like having a roommate who wears your same size. What might feel tired and worn out to one teacher could be a vintage find to another! You may be surprised what another teacher has to offer that is not currently getting any action. Take some time to shop around with your colleagues to add to your supplemental or enrichment collection. Finally, having a supplemental unit to swap out for something that has gone stale for you may be just what you need when summer can't come fast enough. In art class, it may be an outdoor project like chalk designs on the sidewalk or bricks of the building instead of doing something indoors. Maintaining a video archive with optional units allows you the flexibility to make choices for your own mental health and sanity.

### Interactivity

Interactive videos work! A 2018 study concludes that incorporating "interactive learning moments into videos gives students a sense of control and puts them in charge of their learning" (Gedera & Zalipour, 2018, p. 366). But if interactive video lessons sound too techy to tackle, think again. It's easier than you might think. There are web-based programs with free versions for educators, so get ready to have some fun exploring. EdPuzzle (https://edpuzzle.com) is one such program. It allows you to program your own questions on a video, whether it is one you recorded or from some other source, and check data to see which students are watching the videos and for how long. Visit https://youtu.be/5H7zGvgKjbc for a tutorial. PlayPosit (https://go.playposit.com) integrates with many LMS platforms, with options for all grade levels and different prices. Both of these options will help ensure that students are watching, engaging, and learning.

## Recording Specific Subjects and Approaches

The creative, artistic responses to teaching through the pandemic astound me. If I ever feel discouraged and drained, all I need to do is visit the arts classes to recharge my batteries. Theater director Daniel Pronley says his motto through the challenging time was, "Adapt and thrive" (D. Pronley, personal communication, April 3, 2021). Using recording to enhance and improve learning is a prime practice in the world of the arts. From art classes that found improved methods of capturing demonstrations, to choir teachers who used software to compile, blend, and mix musical recordings, to world language teachers who overcame the challenges of evaluating the spoken word, to science teachers who brought experiments to life, to special education teachers who spanned the distance to inspire, to physical education teachers who found ways to inspire fitness from home, to club and artistic directors who found creative ways to blend the physical and virtual worlds, their creativity and resourcefulness are amazing! Not only have teachers adapted to creatively using video in their classroom instruction, extracurricular programs are thriving, too.

Keep in mind that your videos are meant to be helpful, but they don't need to be works of art. The most important goal is to make them useful and accessible to your students. If setting up the perfect recording conditions stresses you out, let it go. Depending on your class and students, you could even make a game by having multiple students record and selecting the best video in the end. Whatever you do, don't let your own self-doubts get in the way of capturing video.

**TEACHER TIP**

## *Visual Arts*

Leave it to the art teachers to lead the way when it comes to creative distance learning solutions. They think about visuals in a way that some other teachers might not. One middle school art teacher shared that it is beneficial to use a live document camera when demonstrating techniques for students (N. Knuth, personal communication, February 1, 2021). This same teacher built an overhead holder for his iPad, which he uses for recording and streaming: "Having the camera positioned over the top of my table helps students see the methods and techniques I teach. I can also zoom in and focus on specific aspects that students need to see" (N. Knuth, personal communication, February 1, 2021). You can see how it works in figure 1.5 (page 44).

Another art teacher finds that creating videos for specific instructions is better than live instruction: "I record demonstrations of metalsmithing techniques that are difficult to see when I demonstrate in front of a room

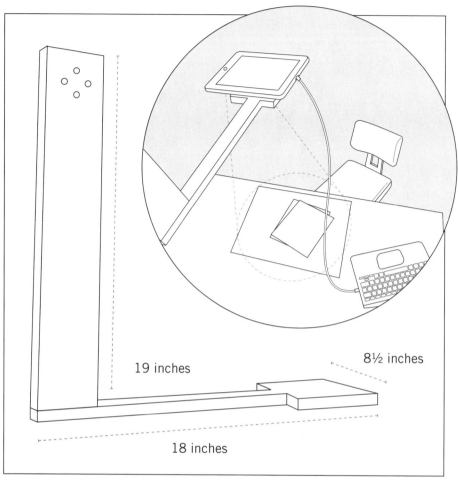

19 inches

8½ inches

18 inches

*Source: Adapted from Nathan Knuth, Wisconsin Hills Middle School, Brookfield, Wisconsin, 2020.*

**Figure 1.5: A handmade tablet holder for overhead recording.**

of thirty students. This way I can zoom in and show students the small details. I delete the sound and [instead do] voice-over" (C. Capriolo, personal communication, February 17, 2021). She explains that students don't have to crowd around to see a demonstration, risking the real possibility that those in the back can't see properly. Recording instructions for techniques has the advantage of zooming the camera to enlarge the focal point of the technique.

An elementary-level art teacher offers other logistical insights, saying that slides alone aren't as engaging for her students and some of her students are just learning to read. Instead, she creates videos on iMovie, incorporating herself discussing the art history or visual elements around which the lesson is based. Then, she demonstrates, directs students, and reviews the lesson (A. Jacobson, personal communication, February 2, 2021).

I teach art metals and have recorded my demonstrations of soldering techniques because it is too difficult for twenty to thirty students to watch me demonstrate this technique to everyone at once. They watch the video when they are ready to learn this technique and take sketch notes on it in their sketchbook. Having students access the videos when they are ready to learn the technique has been very helpful. My art classes have students work at their own pace, so if a student wasn't ready to learn the new technique yet, they don't retain the information if it is presented to the whole group at once. The videos also make it possible for students to go back and review the information as much as they need to.

—**Christine Capriolo, high school art teacher**

By recording lessons and demonstrations, students are still able to continue to work in the shop. Students are able to view videos linked on [our platform] individually or whole group on a large screen.

—**Mark Oelstrom, middle school technology teacher**

**TEACHER**
**VOICES**

## *Music and Theater*

Choir, band, and orchestra are, by their natures, collective, communal experiences. COVID-19 made that impossible, so high school choir teacher Allison Hickman turned to video. She oversaw the creation of a video compilation that blended individual student videos to create one collective video:

Choir and
orchestra
concert[9]

> *We had audio tracks made of the piano accompaniment for each voice part. Then students, on their own time at home, recorded themselves singing their part along with the audio track playing in their headphones [not recorded]. It's not an easy thing to sing a choral piece alone; some students told me they made ten or fifteen videos before they were satisfied with the result. They then submitted their videos to me, and I shared them with our audio mixer to combine and mix and balance the audio tracks. The theater director [combined] their videos into one [and synced] up their videos with the final audio track. (A. Hickman, personal communication, April 7, 2021)*

The accompanying QR code takes you to a video of the recorded concert.

## STUDENT VOICES

In choir and orchestra classes, we turned to livestreamed performances and recording sessions [during the COVID-19 pandemic] in order to share our work, and my teachers put the same work and emphasis behind those as with traditional concerts. Though not able to share our music or convene in the same venues, my music teachers have fearlessly navigated the virtual stage to provide a meaningful musical experience for us.

**—Twelfth-grade student**

**Conducting band**[10]

Band and orchestra programs can integrate videos creatively into instruction with demonstration tutorials, teaching about different instruments and their various parts and sounds, including tips for producing the best sound. Many music teachers took advantage of the resources readily available on the internet. Mark Ramthun, a high school band director, shared that he used videos with students so they could do listening exercises because "to become a better musician, you need to have a concept of what the best of the best actually sound like on their instrument" (M. Ramthun, personal communication, April 9, 2021).

This same teacher made videos of himself conducting to music that he was putting together for a concert: "Students used it as a backing track to play along with as they recorded their part," much the way as described earlier (M. Ramthun, personal communication, April 9, 2021). In addition to creating a conducting video that students viewed while recording their own parts, he also created video tutorials to demonstrate how to do the recordings and upload them for him to use in a compilation. The QR code on this page takes you to a video of the teacher conducting band. Ultimately, music teachers found ways to use both live performances recorded on stage and videos of prerecorded video blends to create spectacular concerts.

In theater, rather than having big initial rehearsals with all cast members learning blocking and choreography, videos give cast members a chance to practice before group rehearsals even begin. For students who struggle to memorize blocking and choreography, having a recording means they can slow down, watch, and practice on their own until they gain mastery.

## *World Languages*

World language classes also rely on sound. Ann Archibald, a middle school Spanish teacher, explains that because capturing and maintaining her students' attention is a real challenge, she designs videos with preteen brains in mind. She starts lessons with an attention-getting hook, keeps lessons brief, and "changes virtual backgrounds weekly to tie into the cultures and histories of the Spanish-speaking world" (A. Archibald, personal communication, February 2, 2021).

**Mandarin Chinese language lesson**[11]

Mary Mann, a high school French teacher, says that having a good microphone is key to creating high-quality videos for her students. She uses a slideshow with text to reinforce language and adds that being visible in the corner of the screen gives students a "chance to see how I am moving my mouth to make the necessary sounds" (M. Mann, personal communication, February 1, 2021). Having students record themselves "worked brilliantly. Timid students were able to do it and redo it until they were satisfied," and distance learners "didn't cut in and out. The emphasis was on presentation and pronunciation (not spontaneous discourse), and it was a great tool" (M. Mann, personal communication, February 1, 2021).

Teaching some languages presents more challenges than others. For instance, teaching Mandarin Chinese to English speakers can be particularly difficult because the spelling and verbal pronunciations are so different from English. One high school Mandarin Chinese teacher, Junfang Lan, shares that teaching in a COVID-19–era hybrid classroom is challenging because she has relied on simultaneously writing and speaking so that students could make the connections between the written and spoken word in the language (J. Lan, personal communication, March 6, 2021). Wearing a mask made this impossible, as the students could no longer see her mouth as she spoke. Creating tutorial videos in a safe environment without wearing a mask allowed her to preteach her lessons and present the videos during the class period. The students could see her write and speak, and she was free to monitor the learning during class. The QR code on this page takes you to a video of the teacher teaching Mandarin Chinese.

## *Sciences and Other Lab-Based Classes*

Science experiments are prime examples of hands-on learning. Video tutorials can take that learning to a higher level. Just like with art, demonstrating a lab in person is limiting because of space issues; not all students can see what is going on. It can also be time-consuming to do these demonstrations, but neuroscience and behavioral professor Robert A. Wyttenbach (2015) explains that "creating videos beforehand, which students can watch

**PE tutorial**[12]

before class and review during lab sessions, solves both of these problems." With the right equipment, such as a high-definition video recorder and microscope adapter, a teacher can record video showing microscopic details that students may have trouble seeing in a large group. Uploading to a site that allows other students to view and respond to your preloaded questions maximizes learning.

Lab work and experimentation lend themselves well to video tutorials and lessons. Like the French teacher who discovered the effectiveness of having students record speeches for pronunciation evaluation, one physics teacher uses the same approach when having students share experiments. In addition to getting feedback and questions about their work, peer assessment "can improve overall learning" (Center for Teaching Innovation, n.d.b). Additionally, when students record their work, they can work simultaneously (instead of the teacher rotating through the class and students waiting for their turn).

### Physical Education

Videos can even improve physical education. And why not? The online fitness industry is booming with everything from yoga to spin classes. Physical education (PE) teachers have found creative ways to both teach and assess their students using video. High school PE teacher Joel Nellis creates videos of himself at home to guide students through home fitness both inside his house and outside, when weather permits. Students are able to watch demonstration videos of their actual teacher to learn proper techniques. On the flip side, students can record themselves completing the exercises rather than only recording an exercise log. The QR code on this page takes you to a PE video tutorial for tempo squats.

Nellis says, "It has worked best to physically demonstrate a movement or exercise. If I need to, I can voice instructions on a video that I create with the movements" (J. Nellis, personal communication, February 1, 2021). Lighting and camera angles are important so students can "see the range of motion or spacing of the exercise" (J. Nellis, personal communication, February 1, 2021). Nellis adds that recording ahead of time, instead of recording an actual class period, allows him to stop and restart a recording, which is sometimes necessary. The text in the left column in figure 1.6 shows links to videos of the teacher showing how to do these exercises.

Teaching students to work out with the resources available in their own homes may be the best instruction they could receive to cultivate a lifetime of personal fitness. Students need time to prepare what they need in order to participate, and sharing videos allows students ample time to find the necessary space and equipment.

|  | Week Four | | |
|---|---|---|---|
| **Exercise** | **Set** | **Rep** | **Notes** |
| Body weight squat and push-ups | 4 | 15 | |
| Single-leg dead lift and chair dips | 4 | 10 | |
| Stair jumps and inverted row | 3 | 10 | Be creative |
| Single-leg calf raises, front and lateral raises | 3 | 15 | Milk jugs or laundry detergent bottles |
| Core | 5 minutes | | Your choice |

**Figure 1.6: Links to exercise demonstrations in the left column.**

## Using Video for Professional Growth

While each district in each state may have its own criteria for assessing professional growth, evidence of excellent teaching is a key component for every teacher to gather. Actual video of your classroom engagement is key evidence of your professional skills and delivery as a teacher.

Whether you are building evidence to add to a portfolio for an annual review or just sharing a lesson with a teaching and learning specialist for coaching, having a wide range of sample classroom videos will help you provide substantial material for others to review. These videos can work both ways with your colleagues, whether you are seeking feedback on your instruction or seeking examples from others. If you are wondering how to teach a concept or someone else is wondering how you do it, sharing videos with colleagues facilitates effective formative feedback.

Unless your material is outdated or you have a better version of the same material, there is no reason to delete videos that you prefer to use if you store them on YouTube. The key to managing the archive is to create an organizational system that works for you. However, you may need to reorganize occasionally. For example, if a tried-and-true unit has lost its appeal, simply slide it into a supplemental folder.

**TEACHER TIP**

**Five-minute video: Literary analysis[13]**

# Try This

Earlier in the chapter, I introduced one of my most impactful discoveries—the five-minute video. I intentionally use a recording format that automatically stops at five minutes so that I am mindful about using my time wisely. For most rational and busy people, a limited time format of five minutes is just short enough to be worth the time it takes to watch for specific information, but if you plan carefully, you can pack it full of substantial material. If it takes longer than five minutes to watch, people might be tempted to try to figure out the content (assignment details, a club update, test review advice, or similar) on their own in some other way. With the promise of *only five minutes* in the title—Five-Minute Pythagorean Theorem Tutorial, for example—more viewers are likely to give it a chance. Pack it full of punch by adding links to a slideshow for reference. Having a concise, well-planned slideshow will help you fit everything you need into the video. The QR code on this page takes you to a five-minute video.

The beauty of the five-minute video, however, is that as the creator, you can pack it full of information in a manageable, organized, easy-to-navigate manner. The following steps reveal the secret to my five-minute-video sauce.

1. Create a slideshow with the bare bones of the information you want to share.

2. Add links to additional resources: documents, web resources, review videos, and other teacher-created videos and materials. For example, I have a video about tips for writing a literary analysis. It has links to the online source that gives examples of literary terms. I also have a video for club fundraising. On the slideshow in that video, I include a link to a sample email script for approaching donors, as well as several links to specific fundraiser information documents.

3. Record yourself presenting the slideshow. You can record yourself on the webcam to give it a more personal feel, showing you speaking and the presentation (side by side or with the webcam in a corner of the screen). Screencastify works for this type of video. It gives you Screen Only and Webcam and Screen options.

4. Insert the link to your recorded presentation on the slideshow's title page. Keep in mind that while the presentation will be visible in the video, the viewer can't click the links while watching. You will need to share the *presentation*, along with the video, for viewers to have access to the embedded links. An

easy way to share both the slideshow and the video at once is to include the video link on the title page of the slideshow. That way the viewer can watch the video and return to the slideshow to access the active links.

5.    Share the slideshow.

With a click, students, parents, guardians, colleagues, and administrators have access to your full presentation (both video and slides), including all the important links embedded in it. They can follow the video directions, starting and stopping at their own pace to access the important links.

## Conclusion

If what you are doing in your classroom holds value, then it is worth recording. Sharing that experience with your current and future students, parents and guardians, administrators, and colleagues reinforces that you believe in your professional abilities and delivery. If you suspect something might be of value but you are not certain, record it! You can always delete the file, but you may not get another opportunity to capture it. As you create and use a video archive, improving student experience and learning, you duplicate yourself, freeing you to focus on other teaching demands.

---

[1] *Debate instruction:* www.youtube.com/watch?v=oMHnkKRD__4

[2] *Thesis statement instruction:* www.youtube.com/watch?v=DLskvgI_HcU

[3] *Enhancement tutorial:* www.youtube.com/watch?v=o9wNJ78S2GY

[4] *Physics enrichment:* www.youtube.com/watch?v=0roQUZvU-As&t=5s

[5] *Chapter reading:* www.youtube.com/watch?v=tRVYeuTlcUI&t=4s

[6] *Whole-class review session:* www.youtube.com/watch?v=zg-fVq-inRU&t=1s

[7] *Lecture:* www.youtube.com/watch?v=sX8yYWFxlHo&t=8s

[8] *Group presentation:* www.youtube.com/watch?v=7N3v7PhekaA&t=3s

[9] *Choir and orchestra concert:* www.youtube.com/watch?v=KoR1cwkyofo&t=9s

[10] *Conducting band:* www.youtube.com/watch?v=2vz2q_OZLEE&t=9s

[11] *Mandarin Chinese language lesson:* https://www.youtube.com/watch?v=JS0zjM1TGEw

[12] *PE tutorial:* www.youtube.com/watch?v=fvY2Y50s8R0

[13] *Five-minute video: Literary analysis:* www.youtube.com/watch?v=wiwcDXpmn_E&t=10s

## Chapter 2

# Preparing Before the Students Arrive

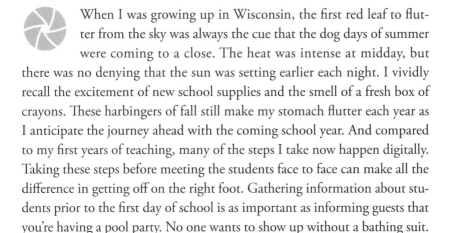When I was growing up in Wisconsin, the first red leaf to flutter from the sky was always the cue that the dog days of summer were coming to a close. The heat was intense at midday, but there was no denying that the sun was setting earlier each night. I vividly recall the excitement of new school supplies and the smell of a fresh box of crayons. These harbingers of fall still make my stomach flutter each year as I anticipate the journey ahead with the coming school year. And compared to my first years of teaching, many of the steps I take now happen digitally. Taking these steps before meeting the students face to face can make all the difference in getting off on the right foot. Gathering information about students prior to the first day of school is as important as informing guests that you're having a pool party. No one wants to show up without a bathing suit.

As criterion for deciding what to record, consider if a recording will help students learn better, either now or in the future. If you are wondering where to begin, "Hello" is a pretty good place to start. Establishing a positive first impression is crucial to creating positive teacher-student relationships. In light of the fact that authenticity is one of the most important factors in building trusting teacher-student relationships, consider introducing yourself and naming some of your favorite things (Bruney, 2012). It sets a positive tone and invites students to share, as well. Ask the students to record themselves talking about their favorite things, too. If they do create reciprocal videos, that is an easy way to gather details and get to know your students before diving into the course content.

While there are many tasks at the start of a new term, getting organized virtually frees you for other demands once students arrive. Remember, this is what works for me. What works for you might be an iteration of this or something different altogether.

This chapter will help you do the following.

- Get permission from administration.

- Start with a checklist.

- Set up your communication platform.

- Choose and set up your video-hosting platform.

- Set up an FAQ.

- Communicate with students, parents, and guardians.

- Gather your equipment and prepare technology.

- Lay the groundwork for an archive.

## Get Permission From Administration

Be sure to check with your administration about any legal concerns they may have before you begin your video archive. For example, you may need to collect permission slips from parents to record their children. Specific students may be on the "no media" list because their parents do not want their children's likenesses used in school resources. It is important to determine who needs to remain out of videos. Just because someone has opted out of appearing in media, however, does not mean that you can't create tutorial videos or record in your classroom. You can adapt, so don't get discouraged. If you need to persuade your administrator that recording in your classroom is worthwhile, consider sharing the benefits for students and teachers (page 5).

Most parents are supportive of video recordings when they understand that the purpose is to help their children learn. Limiting access to videos is an effective way to address most privacy concerns. Adjusting viewing settings to private and sharing only with parents, guardians, and colleagues limits the possible public viewing of the class. Make sure to use a platform that allows that accessibility setting. If some parents still object, it is possible to record without capturing a particular student or group of students. Determining which students are not allowed in the videos before you start recording will prevent you from needing to edit out images or voices. One other option is to record yourself reading or providing steps for projects and guiding questions outside of class.

Figure 2.1 is a video recording permission form you may use to secure needed permissions at the beginning of the year. Check with your administrator to ensure this is acceptable, or if there is a district form you should use instead. You can use it as a written permission slip for parents to sign.

Dear parent or guardian,

Your child is a student in my class this term or year. One of the ways I help students who are absent or need learning support is by occasionally recording my classroom. The recordings are posted on our class calendar, which is accessible only by permission to students in the class, their parents and guardians, support teachers, and future students and parents. No names will appear in any written material about the recording.

The following form will be used to document your knowledge of this activity and to grant or deny your permission for your child to appear on the video recording.

Sincerely,

- - - - - - - - - - - - - - - - - - - - - - - - - - - - - - - - - - - - - - - - - - - - - - - - - - - - - - - -

Teacher name: _____ Date: _____

Student name: _____

I am the parent/legal guardian of the child named above. I have received and read your letter regarding the classroom video recordings and agree to the following: (Please check the appropriate blank below.)

_____ I DO give permission for my child to appear on a video recording and understand my child's name will not appear in any material written about the recording.

_____ I DO NOT give permission for my child to appear on the video recording.

Parent or guardian signature: _____

Date: _____

Figure 2.1: Video recording permission form.

*Visit **go.SolutionTree.com/technology** for a free reproducible version of this figure.*

If you have a virtual platform, you may be able to collect permission slips electronically. Again, be sure to check with your school or district administrator to determine whether this form is sufficient. Some schools may have their own forms they prefer to use.

**TEACHER TIP**

Check your district's policy for recording and posting, and plan accordingly.

If it's allowed:

1. Create or procure the necessary permission slips and have them signed.

2. Post and share the videos.

If it isn't allowed:

1. Record videos of yourself providing instruction alone to share with students.

## Start With a Checklist

Making a checklist or using the one in figure 2.2 can empower you prior to the start of your next term. A checklist can help stave off the feeling that you might be forgetting something. These tasks are in addition, of course, to the myriad things you do in preparation for every new year, such as create your syllabus. I explain some of the tasks in this checklist in this chapter, and others I address in chapter 3 (page 85). Phone apps such as AnyList (www.anylist.com) make it easy to go digital with your checklist.

**TEACHER TIP**

Inserting hyperlinks makes it even easier for people to access your videos because all they have to do is click the text (versus typing in the website address). How you make the address a hyperlink depends on what program you're using, but first try highlighting and then right-clicking the address to see if an appropriate option comes up. If not, look for options such as Insert or icons that look like chain links.

There are no absolutes for the checklist, but these have served me well and will help you start. Be flexible, add, and modify as you go. Before starting a new course, you might find it helpful to preview the units (or asking someone else to preview the units) with the mindset of where it would be

| Complete | Task |
|---|---|
|  | Pair course content, assignments, skills, and assessments with (potential) recordings. |
|  | Create FAQ for course, ensuring links to the communication platform, legal information about recording, and recording purposes are given. |
|  | Invite colleagues of like courses to visit LMS course. |
|  | Record welcome videos for students and for parents and guardians. |
|  | Send welcome email and video and survey to students. |
|  | Send welcome email and video to parents and guardians. |
|  | Send video instructions and permission form to students—video and text versions. |
|  | Send video instructions and permission form to parents and guardians—video and text versions. |
|  | Create (or make a copy of a previous term's) and share week-at-a-glance document with students, parents, and guardians. |

**Figure 2.2: Checklist for start of term.**

*Visit* **go.SolutionTree.com/technology** *for a free reproducible version of this figure.*

helpful to add tutorials and classroom videos. Try to anticipate students' needs and think back on when you have taught the unit in the past, and where students struggled most. In some cases, you might be able to use videos created for one course in another. For example, for my unit on research, I rely on a tutorial that explains how to do an advanced search for sources on the school databases.

Well-meaning and far more organized teachers than I send great ideas via email to our full staff all the time. The good idea train can sometimes feel like it will run you over if you aren't careful, though! When the tips are coming too fast to process, but you know you are going to want that information

**TEACHER**
**TIP**

continued ▶▶

**TEACHER TIP**

someday (maybe even soon), create your own pause button by taking one simple step: create an email folder for tech tips. That way, when you finally realize you need those directions but can't remember who sent them or when, you don't have to dig through hundreds of emails to find help. This can help reduce anxiety. Even the most organized and proficient professionals can become overwhelmed with information overload. Organizing incoming tips and advice in a place where you can access them when you are ready will give you peace of mind. You may not be ready to process great advice when it comes your way, but if you store it in a convenient spot, you can reference it when ready.

At least once every two weeks, dig into that folder and extract key tips and information into a digital notebook. That makes the information more accessible than sorting through email in a folder, trying to remember who sent that one thing that one time.

## Set Up Your Communication Platform

You communicate with students several ways—during class, by individual and group emails, via reminder apps, and more. It is also important to have a central communication hub for the whole class and their families. I have found that a virtual calendar is the most efficient way to share important information, resources, and video links with the class. For me, this is a Google slideshow that I call the *week at a glance*. (The QR code on the next page links to a video that explains how to use the week at a glance.) This is a schoolwide requirement for me. To add an extra layer of security to videos, you can upload them to YouTube or Vimeo so that you have them saved in multiple places. Privacy settings are easy to adjust, and the links are easy to share.

I separate each week of every course on my week at a glance into a separate slide with a block for each day of the week and a sidebar for class information such as my contact information, the Zoom link, course objectives, attendance questions for fun, and links to any related material. For example, if I am teaching a novel, I may add a link to the PDF and one to the study guide. Visit **go.SolutionTree.com/technology** for a free list of attendance questions of the day. This central hub is easy to share. I share the link to the document with students, parents, and guardians. This is a living document, meaning that I add to it regularly. I preload the days that I have video to share, but I also record the actual class period and add that video link to the document at the end of the day. That way, if a student wants to view exactly what happened in class that day, it is available. The preloaded videos are generally shorter and more content focused. For example, I may have a recording of a specific chapter reading, but that is not all that happens in the class period.

**Tutorial:
Using week at
a glance**[14]

If you are using the week-at-a-glance template, it is easy to rearrange the slides so that the current week is always the first slide. Our district uses Canvas, and the template is the home page for my courses. When I work on the document in Google, it automatically updates on the Canvas site. If you don't use Canvas or a similar LMS, share the file another way—just be sure to communicate with students and parents to reference it daily to see what is happening in the class. For example, you can shift the slides so the current week is the first slide, then reshare the week-at-a-glance template with students and parents by 6:00 a.m. every Monday morning. This lets students and parents know what's coming up and plan accordingly (such as, for example, knowing what videos to watch if they miss class).

In the example in figure 2.3 (page 60), the links send students directly to information they need. In the contact information area, there are links to documents: my late work policy, the PDF of the book we're reading, the study guide, and discussion questions. In each day's area on the template, there are links to videos and other resources: recordings of our online Zoom classes, a survey they are asked to complete, and recordings of me reading the assigned chapters, providing tutorials about how to send an assignment by email, and explaining a roundtable.

The different learning management systems that districts choose vary widely in terms of features and change frequently. Recognizing that the playing field can change from one year to the next and taking action to protect your materials will give you the home field advantage for teaching. Whatever you do, make sure that you are saving your videos somewhere in addition to the platform itself. Whether you are saving materials to your district's server, Google Drive, a thumb drive, or the cloud, save frequently and save to multiple places. Getting to know the many facets of your district's platform is key to maximizing its potential and your effectiveness as an educator.

| **Teacher:** Linnihan |
|---|
| **Contact information**<br>linnihan@teacher.k12.school.edu<br>room 212<br>Office hours: Tuesday through Friday from 2:15 p.m. to 3:00 p.m.<br><br>Late work policy<br>Full text of the book we're reading<br>Study guide<br>Discussion questions |
| **Class:** Writing for College, period 3 |
| **For the week of:** April 6–April 10 |
| **Attendance questions:**<br>Monday: None<br>Tuesday: What's the best thing about living in Wisconsin?<br>Wednesday: What course would you like to see added to the school?<br>Thursday: What is the best book or short story you've ever had to read?<br>Friday: What is something good that happened this week? |
| **Weekly learning targets:**<br>"Produce clear and coherent writing in which the development, organization, and style are appropriate to task, purpose, and audience." |

| **Monday, April 6** | No school |
|---|---|
| **Tuesday, April 7** | Zoom recording<br>Introduction<br>Complete survey<br>Journal: If you had another hour in a day, how would you spend it?<br>Email tutorial: Thank-you letter due on LMS at start of class tomorrow |
| **Wednesday, April 8** | Zoom recording<br>Complete survey<br>Journal: If you were in charge, what would you immediately change?<br>Discuss and set schedule for roundtable<br>Read chapter 1 |
| **Thursday, April 9** | Zoom recording<br>Quiz<br>Journal: If you found an animal in the street, what would you do?<br>Discuss chapter 1<br>Read chapter 2 |
| **Friday, April 10** | Zoom recording<br>Quiz<br>Journal: Write a note to a teacher who inspired you, saying how you have used what they taught you in your life currently.<br>Discuss chapter 2<br>Read chapter 3 |

*Source for standard: NGA & CCSSO, 2010.*

Figure 2.3: Week-at-a-glance template.

*Visit **go.SolutionTree.com/technology** for a free reproducible version of this figure.*

## Choose and Set Up Your Video-Hosting Platform

It's important to move your files from your computer to an online location, or you will quickly fill the storage space on your computer. Keep in mind that if you upload to YouTube (www.youtube.com) with your district email login, your videos will stay live on the site, but you may not have access to editing them if you leave the district. Consider uploading to a personal YouTube account to retain access to your videos (provided you have permission to do so). My district does an automatic purge of videos stored in the Zoom folders periodically, so make sure you are saving to a location that won't be wiped clean.

Which platform you choose may come down to personal preference. I use YouTube because there are no limits to how many videos I can upload, and I am not overly concerned about video quality. Some teachers prefer using Vimeo (https://vimeo.com) because they consider the video quality superior. Both sites have video editing tools and links that are easy to share. You may be charged for higher-quality-video hosting sites.

## Set Up an FAQ

Setting up a frequently asked questions (FAQ) doc for each class and linking to the class' landing page is a great way to keep everyone in the loop. Chances are that if a student, parent, or guardian has a question, someone else is wondering the same thing. Adding video responses to the questions makes the communication more personable. You know the kinds of questions you get: I am late with this assignment, but can I still get credit? What is your grading scale? When can we meet for a conference? You can also create FAQs for different units. Units with lots of resources or novel approaches, or complex activities or projects that include many steps and processes are good candidates for these FAQs. If students are asking a lot of questions that you think everyone should hear, it's FAQ time. If you change a policy, or if something changes in the way that you instruct the unit, update your responses on that document and in your recordings.

Some units are smooth sailing, but others generate so many logistical questions that you begin to question if they are worth the trouble. I've found that the ones that push me to the breaking point are the ones that are the most memorable for the students, however. The unit that used to challenge me the most was the whole-class debate. The class was divided in half to debate an assigned topic, and students took the reins with researching, preparing speeches, collaborating, strategizing, and preparing traditional evidence cards. It was fresh territory for them, and each team approached

**FAQ**[15]

the tasks in a unique way. This meant that I gave instructions as needed in their discovery process. Some teams immediately asked questions about argument strategy, while others focused more on gathering evidence at that point in time.

Because the two halves of the class were directly competing with each other, they wanted to be secretive. They drew me into closed team sessions rather than saying their strategies aloud in front of the whole class. Creating an FAQ allowed the students to find answers without involving a full-class discussion, and future students continue to benefit from the questions and answers. Using video for quick responses and tutorials meant that they had my instruction, but were not bound to traditional classroom delivery. Many students tend to pull late nights, so that asynchronous help met them where they were! This unit set in motion the perfect competitive conditions for motivated students. The QR code on this page has an FAQ about debates.

**STUDENT**
**VOICES**

Most of the videos that I watched acted as a foundation for completing my work. The videos showed me where everything for the assignment could be found, and how to start your assignment to ensure success.

—**Tenth-grade student**

**TEACHER**
**VOICES**

The recorded instructions or strategies allow me to meet with my students more often because I am not taking time to explain a math game in class, for example.

—**Heidi Byer, fourth-grade teacher**

In unit-specific documents, I typically insert appropriate headings for the unit. For example, a research unit's headings would be Choosing a Topic, Finding Research, Writing Notes, Rough Drafts and Peer Edits, Final Draft, and Works Cited. Under each heading, students write questions to which I respond in both written and video format. Formatting the document chronologically for the unit keeps order to the responses so that students can easily navigate and find the answers they need. I ask students to highlight their questions when they add them to the document so that I can easily scan it and see what I need to address.

## Communicate With Students, Parents, and Guardians

Communication is key to preparing for your class and the students in it. Laying the groundwork for effective communication throughout the school year begins with the student roster. Sadly, less than half of parents and guardians report being very satisfied with communication from and between themselves and their child's teachers; in fact, about 60 percent of parents who have elementary school students do not receive a phone call from their child's teacher (Child Trends, 2018). Being able to reach out to students, parents, and support personnel can make an enormous difference in the success of students. When teachers and families communicate, odds increase by 40 percent that students will be more engaged and complete their homework (Kraft & Dougherty, 2013).

As soon as you have a student roster, get ready to establish lines of effective two-way communication. Admittedly, there have been terms when I felt like I was barely staying ahead of my students because I was drowning in work. The task of sending group communications was daunting because I hadn't taken the time to preload the email addresses (or phone numbers) into classroom groups (such as Fourth Period Parents). I floundered with the basic task of sending reminders about upcoming assessments, for which there were videos waiting to be reviewed. Added to that was the challenge of remembering which support person I should contact for students with special needs. It quickly became overwhelming. Having specific, custom-made communication groups for students, parents, and guardians (including all critical support teachers and aides) improves communications and ensures that everyone will receive essential communication from you every time.

Whether you have a platform that generates the contacts for you, or you have to take the time to dig the contacts out of student files, the time you spend creating email groups will be worth it in the end. Whatever you do, if you find you are repeating the same step for a second time, take the time to fix it. For example, if you do not have a user-friendly platform to easily email parents and guardians from a grading book, find email addresses once, and then do yourself a favor and make the next time easier. Create a group in your email server and label it so you never have to repeat those steps again. It may be worth your time to create a document to copy and paste email addresses for each class. That way, you will never have to track them down again.

Whatever your classroom platform for communication is, make sure your students, their parents, and all related support people know how and where to access it. There are so many ways to connect that sometimes it becomes overwhelming. Just because students or parents are able to connect with you by email does not necessarily mean that it is the best method. You may prefer that all communications come through the platform messenger, the grading server, or a texting app. Many districts set a preferred policy that is helpful for parents to manage. At one point, I had four children in school. It felt like messages were coming from every direction. When I taught middle school, the students were in "houses." As a team, we sent a weekly communication with an update from each of the core subject teachers. Once students hit secondary school, they have multiple teachers, compounding the communication challenge. If you want parents and guardians to engage in communication, simplicity is the key: know where to go for the information!

## TEACHER
### TIP

The week-at-a-glance document is the hub for my courses. It is where I post all links to materials, videos, and assignments. If it is not on my document, we aren't doing it. I caution against posting links in too many places. Distributing materials and links via email, the grading platform, and physical handouts is fine for supplementing, but if you want students and parents to know where to find videos, it's important to direct them to a single location.

Whatever the case, set the ground rules from the very beginning and reliably check for questions at consistent intervals. This will free you from feeling compelled to check multiple platforms to cover all the bases throughout the day. The boundaries may blur easily and quickly. Often, the children of friends and neighbors wind up in my classes. Occasionally, a parent will message me on Facebook or text me instead of using my school email address. Students have even texted questions after getting my phone number from their parents. From texts to your personal phone, to social media direct messages, to Twitter comments and Instagram stories, people find creative ways to connect. Setting clear guidelines from the start will build respectful boundaries and establish more efficient channels of communication. A simple statement on the course syllabus or your introductory video can set the tone: "While we may be connected in social circles, please keep class-related communication to email only. It helps me to stay organized, and I respond to you faster." Don't be afraid to set specific times for access, either. If everyone knows that you make a last check for questions at 5:00 p.m., for example, they will be more likely to prioritize touching base before that time. Just be sure that you clearly communicate what those parameters are.

Transitioning to a completely virtual mode of communication caught most teachers off guard in 2020. Not only did we need to communicate with students, but suddenly the parents had many questions, too. Having a streamlined mode of communication was key to survival. My inbox flooded, and I felt anxious if I wasn't answering quickly enough. As a result, I was spending the majority of my time answering questions from individual emails, and I felt like my actual teaching and grading time took a back burner. Establishing a go-to document for questions and answers saved my time and sanity. Rather than responding with the same information on multiple emails, I shared a Daily Questions document with students and parents. I checked it frequently and found that when I answered questions on the document, the number of emails I received daily plummeted. Going forward, with a bit of editing to remove duplicate questions or to reorder in a more logical way, I have this document to share with my next group of students as an FAQ.

**PANDEMIC**
**PERSPECTIVE**

The following sections explain how to introduce video use, share a full course calendar and a week at a glance, and check on students' at-home technology logistics.

### Introduce Video Use

Videos are worthless if no one knows where and how to access them. Familiarize your class (and their parents and guardians) with the proper steps and provide guidance so they can maximize the benefits of the recordings for their learning. The welcome emails—one for students and, if you're teaching elementary or middle school, one for parents and guardians—will

**Welcome[16]**

be the perfect place to detail specific actions that both groups can take to make the most of the videos. For students, the directions should include guidance for how to do the following.

- Check for available videos related to the classroom content (and where).
- Watch the videos and check the FAQ before asking questions.
- Contact you if questions arise outside of the class period.

For parents, the directions should include guidance for how to do the following.

- Check for available videos related to the classroom content (and where).
- Check the FAQ and view or read them with their child to reinforce classroom learning.
- Contact the teacher (or encourage their child to contact the teacher) if questions arise outside of class.

Some students will need little to no additional support in the process. However, for those parents and guardians who want to be more engaged in their child's learning—and because that and communication between teachers and parents and guardians both affect student achievement—providing access to the resources, including videos, is an inviting way to give full entry to the learning process (Shute, Hansen, Underwood, & Razzouk, 2011). The QR code on this page links to a welcome video for secondary students.

The easier you make the experience, the more likely they are to buy into your classroom communication style. Emphasize your belief in your approach. Figure 2.4 is a checklist you can use to prepare your communications.

**TEACHER VOICES**

My quieter students can see how a problem is solved without having to raise their hands. [Videos also allow] parents to see the problem-solving method so that they can better assist their student.

—**John Wilkinson, high school physics teacher**

| Addressed | Information to Include in Video |
|---|---|
| | **Location:** Record in a well-lit area that is free of noise. If recording a teacher-only video, consider recording in the classroom during a quiet time so students can visualize the space where they will be learning. |
| | **Safety:** Ensure that students' voices and images will be respected and protected. Videos will be shared with current students and support networks with privacy settings secured. |
| | **Permission:** Explain the permission slip that is approved by school administration. Give clear directions about where to access the slip and how and when to return it to you. |
| | **Landing page:** Give clear directions about how to access the Week at a Glance and how to access videos on it. |
| | **Contact preference:** Establish your preferred method of contact and hours for doing so. You may want to insert a slide on the video with your email address, contact hours, and school phone number. |
| | **Why:** Explain why you structure your class this way and use video—to be as good a teacher as possible and improve learning. |

Figure 2.4: Welcome video and communication email checklist.

*Visit **go.SolutionTree.com/technology** for a free reproducible version of this figure.*

## Share a Full Course Calendar and Week at a Glance

For many years, I have used a course calendar as a function of Canvas. It is easy to copy from one course to another, as it adjusts the dates and retains any materials linked to it. This is not unique to Canvas, however. As long as you have URL links on a calendar, you can easily shift the material to fit a new calendar year. Unlike the week-at-a-glance document that shows one week at a time, the calendar gives a bigger picture of what lies ahead. For some students and parents, this gives a clearer perspective than the week at a glance in isolation.

Consider creating a calendar like the one in figure 2.5 (page 68). In this example, there are links to relevant videos (both those created in the classroom and those that students may watch to later discuss). Adjust privacy settings so that students, parents, guardians, and colleagues can view them.

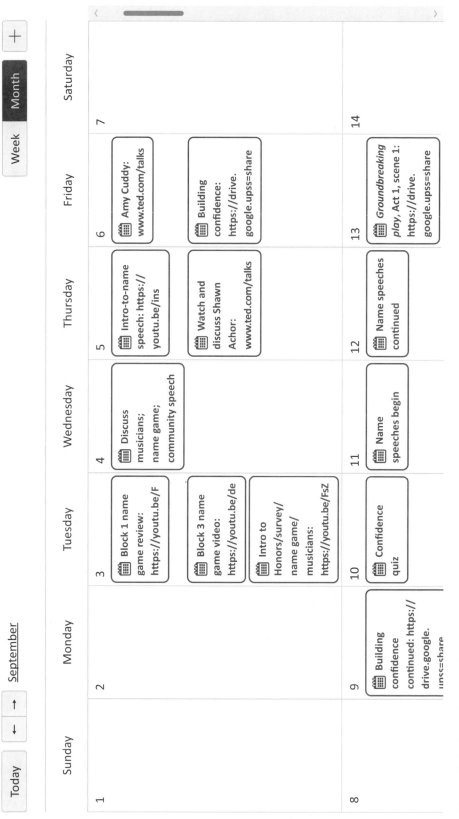

**Figure 2.5: Sample calendar page.**

If your district has a platform, such as Canvas or Schoology, that allows you to copy full courses and calendars from one term to the next, the calendar feature is a great way to manage videos and import all of your planning to the new term. You will likely need to adjust the dates to fit the new term, but essentially, if the content is nearly the same, this is a good starting point, importing the class as a base and tweaking information as needed. I teach in a district that has a block schedule, so my courses begin quarterly rather than just once a year in the fall. When I copy a course from September to a new starting point later in the year, I adjust the dates to fit the new term. Copying a course calendar carries all of the video and content links from one term to another, but be careful to check for accuracy once it's copied over, making sure links function properly.

Although the terms roll out similarly, using the calendar to move video links according to the daily flow of each term can help you be flexible. In your school's LMS, you may be able to click and drag content from one date to another on the calendar. If you don't quite get to something in a class period, simply drag the segment you didn't do to the following day. In this way, the calendar is more of a ballpark planner than a true daily planner, as is the week at a glance. Whether you share access to the calendar or simply use it for your own planning purposes, be sure that both students and parents are aware that it is subject to change. For students who know about upcoming absences, the calendar gives them better control of their planning. Even if you have not yet introduced an upcoming unit, if a student wonders what the class will be doing the week prior to winter break, the calendar provides that. With video links, a student—with coordination and guidance from you—could work ahead, using videos to navigate the material. For younger elementary students, parents may consult the calendar when considering whether it will be manageable for their child if they are considering taking them out of school for various activities.

Smart saving habits mean you can retain all of your planning, archived videos, and resources to take with you if you move to another position in a different school or district. It's important to note that links in a document need to be portable, too. If you copy your week at a glance to a personal drive, that's a great start, but if you do not do the same for the video links that are hyperlinked onto it, you will not have access to those videos once your Google account is deactivated. Keep in mind, also, that permissions do not necessarily travel with you. If you are copying tutorials of yourself only, that is not a problem, but if students appear in your videos, you must secure permission to use those videos for future educational use only. Check with your district about their permission policies.

## TEACHER VOICES

I've been teaching for more than twenty-five years. I know what the students need to know, and I test them on what I want them to know. By creating videos (sometimes recording my classes), I know they are getting the information that I want them to get.

—**John Harder, high school science teacher**

### *Check on Students' At-Home Technology Logistics*

In order for students to access and view videos at home, they need (in addition to electricity) a device (such as a smartphone, tablet, or laptop) and an internet connection. These are not givens for all students, who may be sharing a device with other family members, lack these technologies altogether, have limited bandwidth, or lack an internet connection.

While no one can predict every possible mishap, there are ways to plan for some of the obvious. First, if students have limited access to a device, they may need help coordinating a schedule for using devices. Access to a video archive makes this coordination easy. For example, imagine siblings are trying to use one laptop during scheduled class periods; it is impossible. However, if one can watch videos after the younger siblings have gone to bed, this adds flexibility to the family schedule. Downloading video content in early mornings or late evenings, rather than streaming it during peak hours, can free some bandwidth.

Occasional distance-learning technical bumps make the video archive invaluable. For example, if a student has connection issues, he or she can leave the real-time instruction and watch the video for that day instead until the connection issues are resolved. Establishing a pattern of posting previously recorded classes in an easily accessible location allows students with connectivity issues to access the material in their regularly scheduled time slot. One of my students touched base before leaving on a vacation. She planned to join into the daily online class calls, but for the final day of the trip, she knew she would be on a flight at that time. She informed me that she would download the previously recorded class video for that day and view it on the plane to stay caught up. Obviously, this is a highly functioning student with all the resources she could need, but the potential for all students to be this assertive and well self-managed is very real!

Occasionally, remote learners in my class signal to me through the chat feature that they are having connection issues at home. It is easy enough to have them watch the previously recorded class video posted on the week at a glance for that day instead of suffering through a lagging internet connection. In addition, I create video recordings of each class to post later in the day on the class week-at-a-glance document (figure 2.3, page 60), so students can choose between viewing a previously recorded class or waiting for the daily recording to post. Obviously, missing the live class is not optimal, and being in class is impossible to truly replicate, but having recorded video available as an alternative is the next best solution.

Consider asking students to complete the survey in figure 2.6 (page 72) so you can check their at-home technology logistics. I usually send the survey at the end of the first week so that everyone—both students and I—have a chance to work out the kinks.

## Gather Your Equipment and Prepare Technology

If you are fortunate enough to teach in a district that employs a technology coordinator of some sort, you have hit the jackpot (keeping in mind tech mavens don't always have the bandwidth to support extra projects). Many times I have struggled to figure out how to do something technical, only to find that there is a very simple solution. If following technology trends is not your passion or focus, little problems with it can become overwhelming. Asking a technology coordinator for help brings to light a quick fix. What is challenging for many of us is often common knowledge to someone who speaks the language of technology. They are full of great ideas to make everything run more smoothly and efficiently. I have yet to meet a technology enthusiast who is not exactly that—enthusiastic.

Not sure if such a person exists in your district? Find out. Ask around and soon you'll figure out who the keeper of the knowledge is. He or she may not even hold an official technology title. Maybe it's the biology teacher down the hall. Some people love virtual gadgetry and may be willing to give guidance, provided they have the time. If you strike out finding such a person, there are endless tutorials available online for virtually any type of technology challenge you may have. There are also teaching forum groups on social media sites like Facebook and Twitter.

Some districts offer optional breakout sessions and in-service opportunities at the start of the school year. Generally, these are conducted as workshops where you bring your device and follow along with the instructor, learning and implementing new changes for your own courses. If your district offers in-service related to technology and your district platform,

How well can you hear me in the videos?

|                                              | 1 | 2 | 3 | 4 | 5 |                                              |
|----------------------------------------------|---|---|---|---|---|----------------------------------------------|
| Not well or less than<br>20 percent of the time | ○ | ○ | ○ | ○ | ○ | Very well or more than<br>80 percent of the time |

How well can you see instruction in the videos?

|                                              | 1 | 2 | 3 | 4 | 5 |                                              |
|----------------------------------------------|---|---|---|---|---|----------------------------------------------|
| Not well or less than<br>20 percent of the time | ○ | ○ | ○ | ○ | ○ | Very well or more than<br>80 percent of the time |

What is one thing that I am doing well and should continue doing in the videos?

What is one thing that I should consider doing differently in the videos?

What technology issues are you having?

Figure 2.6: Technical clarity and connectivity survey.

*Visit **go.SolutionTree.com/technology** for a free reproducible version of this figure.*

be sure to attend. I encourage you to find a colleague from your department to attend with you so that you can learn together and be able to consult about the session, if necessary, in the future. Summer seems to be the time that many platforms update and improve their networks. While these changes are supposed to make teaching easier or more efficient, they can also feel overwhelming to a returning teacher when the old familiar platform looks different in the fall. Chances are that you will need to figure out the changes, like it or not, so spending time with someone who has already learned the changes will smooth your task considerably. Facing it alone can be incredibly frustrating, but exploring with a colleague could be enjoyable. The administrator running the session may even be a colleague. Why waste time navigating alone when you can learn from someone who has already figured it out? Take advantage of any professional development opportunities you can with people who spend their days immersed in this subject matter. They are a wealth of knowledge that is often untapped. Again, if your district does not offer these types of learning and training sessions, there are many tutorials available on the internet.

Having your recording tools ready to go is essential to starting your video archive. Fortunately, many people walk through life ready to record with a smartphone. In fact, over 80 percent of Americans own a smartphone (Pew Research Center, 2019); the number is 75 percent in Canada (Georgiev, 2021). A smartphone is all you need for recording—but you have to make sure your district permits teachers to use smartphones in the classroom. Some people may want to invest in a small tripod to stabilize the camera, but propping books works, too.

If you do not have a smartphone, a laptop with a webcam can work, too. This might not be ideal if you need your laptop for other purposes throughout the lesson, however. Another alternative is an actual video camera. Some schools will have these available to check out from the library. If you have a choice, I recommend a camera that uses a Secure Digital (SD) card. This is easy to pop out and insert into a computer port (if it has one) or into an adapter that plugs into your computer. If you're using your phone to record, you may be able to transfer files through your Wi-Fi connection or by connecting your phone or camera directly to your computer. The specific adapter you need will vary depending on your recording device and computer, but you can search online by manufacturer, task, and equipment and find what you need.

The time between first considering making video recordings and actually doing it can sometimes derail even the best intentions. If the decision to record requires multiple steps that take even the smallest amount of time to execute, it is easy to avoid recording because it is inconvenient. The harder you make the job, the more likely you are to avoid it. On the other hand, if recording is as simple as pushing a button on your smartphone, you are more likely to give it a try—even if you do delete it!

If you plan to use a traditional video camera with a tripod, set it up in your classroom as a regular part of the landscape. Having the equipment in full view will remind both you and your students that it is there for a reason, and you will be more likely to use it regularly if you keep it ready to go in your room. Don't let a dead battery or difficult recording angle prevent you from capturing the moments you want to preserve: keep the battery on a charger or position the tripod close to an outlet. Depending on the type of recording you do, you may choose to use different camera angles for different purposes. If you are reading something or leading a discussion, for example, I generally use a wide angle from the back of the room to easily capture all the students and their voices. For a lecture, I use a closer shot just on me and the board. You may find that sound quality is an issue if the angle is too wide when trying to capture the full class, so you may need to move the camera closer. Wearing a voice-amplifying headset could solve that problem. You can use the checklist in figure 2.7 to double-check that all the necessary equipment and requirements for successful recording are ready to go.

Once you have saved videos on your phone or uploaded videos to your computer, the next step is to decide where to put them. Uploading directly to your school platform may work, but be sure to save your videos somewhere else as well. YouTube has privacy settings that allow you to control who can view or share your videos. Google also offers options to save video and control the sharing settings. Whatever option you choose, be sure that you maintain control over your content by setting the privacy settings to your preference. For example, on my school Google account, I can limit access to files for Google email addresses that are only within our district domain. When you share in that program, you will see a prompt that guides you through your preferred settings.

For anyone who wants a slick, all-in-one recording site, there are several good ones. Screencastify (www.screencastify.com) works with Google Chrome and has a user-friendly format (although the free version is limited in time). I find a timing limitation to be the perfect challenge when I am recording a daily announcement or short tutorial. I even include "Five-Minute Update" in the title so that students and parents can see that the videos will be brief. Sometimes that is the perfect enticement to get them to watch! Whichever you choose to use, keep in mind that if you store on the

| Tools |
|---|
| ☐ Video camera |
| ☐ Smartphone |
| ☐ Laptop |
| ☐ SD card (If uploading and then deleting files daily from the SD card, the size is unimportant.) |
| ☐ Charger |
| ☐ Enabled webcam |
| ☐ Power cord |
| ☐ USB cord |
| ☐ Extension cord |
| ☐ Tripod or other camera mount |
| **Computer** |
| ☐ Compatible connector for uploading (SD card port, USB port, or the like) |
| ☐ Internet access for uploading to host site |
| **Optional items** |
| ☐ Podium |
| ☐ White screen, blank wall, or sheet for backdrop (Depending on your purpose, you may have a logo or significant quote in view behind you.) |
| ☐ Other: _____ |

Figure 2.7: Classroom recording checklist.

*Visit **go.SolutionTree.com/technology** for a free reproducible version of this figure.*

site with your school email address, you may not have access to your videos if you move to another district in the future. Taking the time to upload your content to a personal space will ensure that you don't lose it.

## Lay the Groundwork for an Archive

With a video archive, keeping everything organized is essential to benefitting from the potential for time savings. There are several methods that could work for you. Whether you file by date, topic, courses, or some other method, you will likely want to save videos in multiple places. You may even find that you prefer more than one way to archive and organize. As long as you have a system that you can easily navigate for future reference, you are making a time-saving investment in your future. This section discusses traditional filing systems and what to do with special-occasion files.

**Tutorial: Writing on and saving a PDF[17]**

*This is important to note:* since district platforms are dictated by financial contracts, they may have an expiration date. Make sure your intellectual property does not disappear at the end of that date. Ensure that by saving your videos and documents with links to your personal server of choice, preferably on the cloud for safekeeping. It is always wise to inquire about the contract for your district so that you are not caught off guard. Whatever the case may be for your district, creating a document to insert the LMS landing page for your class will be a terrific time saver.

**PANDEMIC PERSPECTIVE**

When I began to build my video archive in 2015, I never imagined the impact it would have on my teaching in 2020. While it was not a seamless transition into virtual teaching for the COVID-19 pandemic, it was as smooth as I could have hoped. With an archive, I could assign specific classroom lessons for my students to watch and then spend virtual office hours answering questions about the lessons. In the early days of the pandemic, when there was little structure to the schoolwide class schedule, I held virtual classes for those who could log on, but I also had office hours every day for students to ask questions. When students were double booked and couldn't attend my class virtually, they were able to watch the recording of a previous term's class instead. Some were juggling work schedules, caring for siblings, and encountering a variety of internet issues. It was a manageable alternative to watch a previously recorded class period instead. Tutorials from previous classes were just as helpful during remote teaching.

Of course, the virtual experience presented even more opportunities to create new tutorials to manage assignments virtually. I found myself recording tutorials about how to record your screen and your webcam at the same time and for writing on a PDF and saving it. While the internet is full of similar content, I wanted to connect personally with my students by showing them some of the logistics myself. (The QR code on this page links to a tutorial about writing on and saving a PDF.)

## *Traditional Filing System*

When I first moved into my classroom, it was lined with gray metal filing cabinets. While I knew there must be hidden treasures in them somewhere, the thought of sorting and purging was daunting. There seemed to be no logical organizational method. Alphabetical is the logical first rule of order, but alphabetize by *what* exactly? The name of the course? The name of the unit? The name of the assignment? In a virtual system, you can file many different ways—chronologically or by course, unit, or assignment—without concern of overstuffing the system.

Looking back at some of my first videos, I realize now that I could have done a better job of organizing myself. Just like a messy desk, a messy drive is equally difficult to navigate when you want to find something. Admittedly, when I first started my archive, there were lessons that I dumped because they didn't fit neatly into a specific set of criteria I had devised. If the video did not capture a full lesson, I would scrap the video and try to get a better recording the next time. Consider the following when you set up an organizing system for videos, as it will help you and your students find them in your archive when needed. I was also completely oblivious to the genius of using folders!

- **Create subfolders for specific types of videos:** You can create subfolders by unit or date, for example. You may want to label by unit, type of activity, or genre.

- **Name videos:** Be as specific as possible when naming videos. You will save yourself time by naming accurately to avoid having to open a video to determine its exact contents.

- **Make copies:** When organizing, make copies of videos to store logically in multiple folders.

Sometimes recordings do not start or end in convenient or logical places for future reference. For example, at times, I have been near the end of a lesson when the bell rings, or I decided the class needed some wiggle time. I typically give a five minute stretch-and-wiggle brain break somewhere near the middle of class. While it is a much-needed break for face-to-face learners, students accessing the video at a later time would not need that. They can simply pause the video at any time. In that case, I may title a video "Macbeth Act 2 beginning–wiggle break." The next video would be "Macbeth Act 2 after wiggle–end." Labeling videos in a specific manner for future reference helps students to find what they need and helps me share content that matches the classroom experience. It took me some time to realize that these organic lessons were authentic to what was happening in my classroom and, thus, exactly what my students needed.

**TEACHER TIP**

It's important to be aware of auto-formatting features. For example, computers automatically categorize numbers first. I worked around this when I set up my folder for Writing for College. After a few days of scrolling to the bottom of my folder list, I renamed the folder 4CW so that it would be at the top. I could also have used characters and renamed the folder _Writing for College, for example.

To start, you may want to create folders in your drive for each course. Then add a folder that can hold contents that applies to *all* of your courses (such as your welcome videos). Other types of videos to store in this spot might be typical how-tos. If you place those types of videos in a specific course, you may have a hard time finding them again. Remember, you should make copies of videos to store in multiple locations. This organization, shown in figure 2.8, works well when a unit is portable from one class to another. For example, I often find room for an extra unit of Shakespeare's (1623/1997) *The Taming of the Shrew* in an English class ranging from freshmen to seniors. Creating a filing system for the videos discussing the play's acts makes those files convenient to find, rather than tucking them into a class labeled by grade level, as shown in the following list. Organizing in this way also makes sharing with colleagues easier because I can share a folder for the unit rather than locating it in a course and sharing files piecemeal. While they may not choose to share the videos with their own students, your colleagues have your teaching method readily available to mentor them through a new unit.

**STUDENT VOICES**

Honors English videos were very helpful for clarification of Shakespeare plays, as they can be a bit difficult to understand and a second listen would usually clarify anything I missed.

—Tenth-grade student

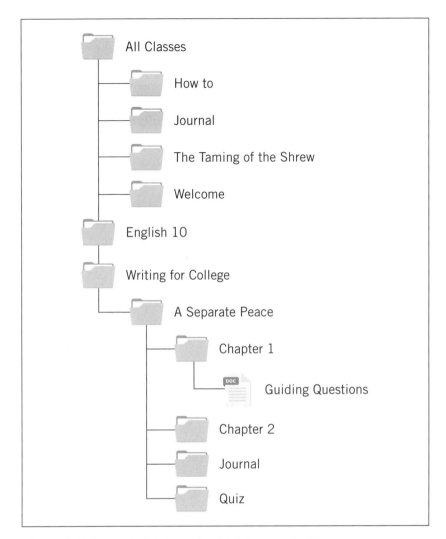

Figure 2.8: Example folder and subfolder organization.

## Special-Occasion Files

Most people don't store holiday decorations in their kitchen cabinets. Whatever holidays you observe, it is likely you have tucked the big containers filled with tidings of the season well out of the way of your home's daily operations. This is because you don't need them every day. Supplemental units for teaching are just like those well-loved decorations. You don't need them all the time, but when you feel that the time is perfect for pulling them out, it is critical that you know where to find them.

How you store supplemental units is key to keeping track of them. If you rely on only copying the calendar, you will not readily see these videos, and you may lose track of them. You may want to create a folder on the cloud or Google Drive that is reserved for the extra material. You can label

**Tutorial: Organizing and sharing a welcome video**[18]

it as Supplemental Materials and add subfolders with it. The QR code on this page links to a video showing you how to organize and share a welcome video.

You can store your videos in multiple ways. For example, you could create one document for an entire unit of study that includes both video links and other materials, like in figure 2.9. This one document could include hyperlinks to videos of instruction of each segment of the unit, as well as links to files of study guides, quizzes, and tests. Saving a document such as this in the unit folder serves as a type of table of contents with live links. Sharing an entire unit with a colleague is as easy as sharing a link. Creating a link to share with students *without* the quizzes and tests is a great way to make navigation easier for them, too. Once I create a document such as this for a unit, I link it on my week at a glance so it is easy for students and parents to find.

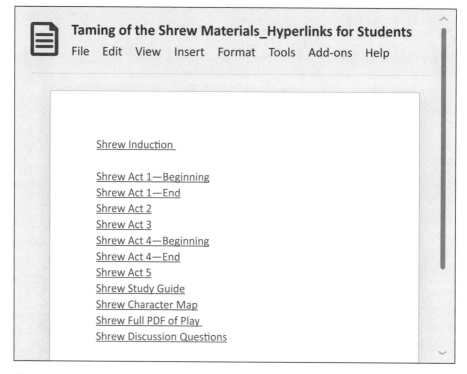

Figure 2.9: Word document with links to videos and other resources for students.

You can also create a separate document with links that go to tests and assessments to share with colleagues, like the one you see in figure 2.10. Just be sure to have your settings open for the embedded links and be careful who you allow and where you send the information when sharing the teacher version.

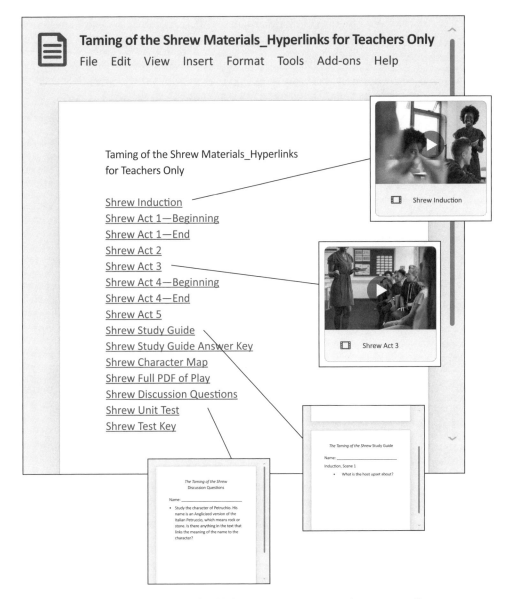

**Figure 2.10: Word document with links to assessment and corresponding videos for teachers.**

Some links in the example go directly to instructional videos and others go to support and assessment materials. You can share an entire unit at once this way. Be sure to check individual links to share with colleagues, as the document on which they are posted won't alter those settings automatically. You will need to change each URL setting to either View or Edit, depending on your preference. I share *only* with viewing access so that someone else does not edit my original documents. Sharing with viewing rights still allows the viewer to make and edit their own copy.

Sharing one document could equate to sharing multiple documents if the settings are open for those contained in the host document. If you share a document with assessments linked to it, be sure that your colleague understands the importance of privacy settings. It's easy to share assessments this way, but it is also easy to accidentally share with students if you are not careful. Sharing that document with students would create more work, with you having to recreate assessments after giving away questions and answers!

This may be the most straightforward, conveniently shared document that you could create to store an entire unit of material. You, students, and colleagues will each have a one-stop shop for all related materials for an entire unit of study. While it takes time to record the videos, upload the documents, and create a single document for sharing everything, it will be worth the time investment for everyone.

## Try This

Checking views and following up with students can provide insight for the teacher as to who may need additional support. To a casual observer, it may appear that everyone is equally engaged in the learning, but what is happening in the classroom is only one component. Students may be unaware that classmates are tapping into virtual outlets of information. For example, a student might think that the only work happening is on hard copy, while other students are monitoring the week at a glance and seeing that there are virtual components to do, as well. For example, there might be a survey to complete on the day's date that does not come on paper. If you have online expectations for participation, students need to know what they are and where to find the materials and assessments.

Even if you feel you have shouted with a megaphone, some students will still miss online components without continual reinforcement. Analyzing views and following up with students who missed the video will smooth the path in the future for more important communications that may affect summative assessment material. In class, demonstrate how to access videos. Show a video in class early in the course. If students are still not accessing the videos, you may need to spend one-on-one time with them to walk through the process. If you have covered this ground in the welcome video, you may want to instruct them to watch that one again.

You can track data about student video use using the following steps.

1.  Create a video that has specific information for a single class. For example, this could be details about a class party, which students would be motivated to watch.

2. Share the video and explain how students can access it.

3. Check the number of views.

If a video created for and shared with a specific class with thirty students has fifty views, in all likelihood most of the students watched it, and some watched it multiple times. If there are very few views in a class, it may not have been particularly helpful or there may be a disconnect for students in accessing the platform. Of course, checking these data isn't a foolproof method, as some students may have watched more than once or twice while others have not watched at all.

Also, this basic information can guide a teacher to provide reinforcement for accessing and viewing the videos on the classroom platform. The more you record and post, the more students will become accustomed to accessing videos to enhance their own learning.

## Conclusion

Setting the stage for a successful school year starts before students arrive in the classroom. Using the prep time wisely will make the year more enjoyable for both your students and *you*. Taking the time to set up the virtual elements of your classroom will provide a window into your actual classroom for students and their support network. Taking the time to ensure that everyone is comfortable and feels welcome goes far toward building effective relationships and instruction. Every step you take before the students arrive—setting up virtual communication, calendars, cameras, and FAQs—will help your students feel welcome in your class. When you have your video camera ready to go, you are more likely to use it. Keep in mind that if something is worth repeating, it is worth recording, so get ready to search for those golden moments. Preparing yourself with a well-organized filing system and the right equipment and conditions to produce meaningful videos will set you in the right direction.

---

[14] *Tutorial: Using week at a glance:* www.youtube.com/watch?v=DLGQ_ZAmN3Y&t=2s

[15] *FAQ:* https://docs.google.com/document/u/0/d/1NpWWp9CjTMO-AnBb6Dgtwihue7mCHJba
　　/mobilebasic#heading=h.gjdgxs

[16] *Welcome:* www.youtube.com/watch?v=tf1H58mAK4E&t=4s

[17] *Tutorial: Writing on and saving a PDF:* www.youtube.com/watch?v=rkeZEoyrOi8&t=1s

[18] *Tutorial: Organizing and sharing a welcome video:* www.youtube.com/watch?v=o8xA1WB1FT8

## Chapter 3
# Building Communication Confidence

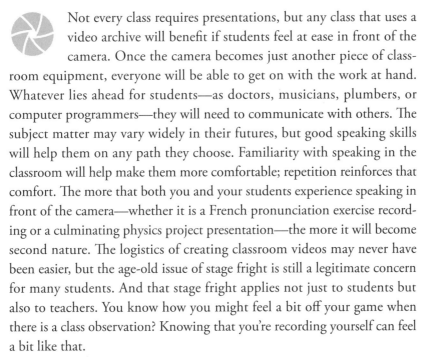Not every class requires presentations, but any class that uses a video archive will benefit if students feel at ease in front of the camera. Once the camera becomes just another piece of classroom equipment, everyone will be able to get on with the work at hand. Whatever lies ahead for students—as doctors, musicians, plumbers, or computer programmers—they will need to communicate with others. The subject matter may vary widely in their futures, but good speaking skills will help them on any path they choose. Familiarity with speaking in the classroom will help make them more comfortable; repetition reinforces that comfort. The more that both you and your students experience speaking in front of the camera—whether it is a French pronunciation exercise recording or a culminating physics project presentation—the more it will become second nature. The logistics of creating classroom videos may never have been easier, but the age-old issue of stage fright is still a legitimate concern for many students. And that stage fright applies not just to students but also to teachers. You know how you might feel a bit off your game when there is a class observation? Knowing that you're recording yourself can feel a bit like that.

This chapter provides ideas for how to do the following.

- Build confidence for teachers
- Build confidence for students

## Build Confidence for Teachers

Teacher confidence matters because the assurance you project impacts your lesson delivery and message; it affects both students and teachers. As psychology scholars Daniela Barni, Francesca Danioni, and Paula Benevene (2019) attest:

> *Teachers' self-efficacy, namely teachers' beliefs in their ability to effectively handle the tasks, obligations, and challenges related to their professional activity, plays a key role in influencing important academic outcomes (e.g., students' achievement and motivation) and well-being in the working environment.*

As the teacher, you set the tone. Model the behaviors you want your students to learn, and soon they will follow suit. If you project an anxious vibe, the students detect that energy and mirror it. Expecting the best of your students begins with expecting the best of yourself. Using video in a casual, confident manner sets the expectation for students to do so, as well.

Using video to honestly critique your own professional delivery is a profoundly effective way to improve teaching. One of the most challenging personal and professional endeavors that I have ever completed was my National Board Certification. The area of growth that made the greatest impression on me and pushed me to be a better version of myself was the component that required video submissions of my teaching. From the moment that I learned of the task, my head began swimming with the possibilities. Choosing which lessons to record and submit was only the beginning. Throughout the experience, I considered every possibility and recorded significantly more lessons than I was required to analyze and submit. Working on the certification was a quest that kept me continually challenging myself: Is this the best lesson to use? Could it be better? It is amazing how much I improved in both my delivery and efficiency in my pursuit of excellence. Whatever your personal goals for teaching are, taking the time to reflect on recordings of your lessons will open your eyes to many possibilities for improvement.

Because reviewing oneself on video is often extremely uncomfortable to do, give yourself some guidelines to be objective. Taking inventory of your skills involves personal conviction but is related to autonomy, which "promotes mastery because autonomous individuals care enough to master the knowledge and skills that are likely to elevate the work they believe in" (Tomlinson, 2019). Educators must be willing to hone their delivery skills (especially if they're asking students to do the same). You can even apply the rubric that your administrator will use to do formal evaluations of you on your own self-analysis. Just as we teach students to use our own rubrics to prepare for their assessments, practicing this same behavior will help you to cover the necessary ground you will need to present for a positive review.

Spend some time looking at the criteria for a classroom observation that an administrator might use to evaluate you. Doing this informally to prepare on your own can strengthen your confidence and reassure you that you are covering the ground that will make it a good lesson worthy of recording.

**Computer display with voice narration**[19]

Logically, there is no reason to be fearful of making a recording that you can easily delete if you dislike it. The problem is that logic does not necessarily govern our bodies and brains. Even though we are mature enough to behave in a civilized manner, we are wired at a primitive level for the fight, flight, or freeze response. So, while you are not likely to run and hide at the sight of a camera in the same manner that you might on encountering a bear in the woods, your internal response still feels a sense of panic when you feel threatened in any way. For many, the thought of recording is frightening. According to psychology scholars Danielle J. Maack, Erin Buchanan, and John Young (2015), "Fear is a basic emotion which functions to promote avoidance goals by assisting in escape from threats (flight and freeze) or defensive approach (fight) in situations where avoidance is not an option" (p. 117). Facing the unknown in a camera lens can trigger this response. Like the proverbial monster under the bed, our adversary is not in plain sight, and it triggers our imaginations to run wild.

In the next sections of this chapter, I address the following confidence-building strategies for teachers.

- Starting small
- Focusing on why you're recording
- Pressing delete if it doesn't pass muster
- Self-evaluating and getting and giving feedback

### Starting Small

If recording your face makes you feel inauthentic or too nervous to deliver content in a natural manner, consider starting with a recording of a computer-screen-only tutorial. In this type of video, which you can do on Zoom or Screencastify, you can record your computer display with or without your voice narration. This works well for tutorials in which you are instructing students on how to do something on their own computers. For example, I use my voice when I demonstrate how to access the school library databases. When I show it in class, I use the SMART Board to display the video so that students can use their own devices to walk through the steps with me in real time. The QR code on this page takes you to a video of a computer screen display with voice-over.

Students can demonstrate learning with the same type of recordings. Consider designing an assignment in which students create a similar type of video that displays their own screen. From a first-grade report about a frog's life to a twelfth-grade report about the environmental impact of pollutants on fish, using video will bring projects to life. It is also far more valuable for the whole class to experience the video reports than for just the teacher to read a hard copy, as everyone can learn something new this way. You can assign it as asynchronous work outside of class. This is a built-in feature in Canvas and Flipgrid, as well as many other programs.

You can also start behind the camera by recording a student-led activity in class or as an assignment. Once everyone gains more confidence with the recordings, you can advance to recording your lectures and student presentations in class. In my experience, most students are quite comfortable with recording immediately, but some others may take a few weeks. Group or partner work is a comfortable way to ease students into recordings, too. They tend to feel more relaxed if they are not alone. Recording frequently for all types of activities (not just assessments, such as final presentations for a project or graded speeches, that may impact students' nerves) is a great way to familiarize both yourself and your students with using videos to enhance learning. When students are focused on the lesson—an art demonstration followed by hands-on participation, a gym class basketball unit when they are working on layups, or a one-hundred-days-of-school celebration when kindergarteners count their one-hundred objects—they are not likely to care about the camera.

Also keep in mind that just because you record something, you're not required to use it in the future. Just as a photographer may take fifty shots to get one or two great ones, you may find that you keep only a small percentage of the recordings you make. Unlike a photographer, however, you are not shooting for perfection. If there is educational value in what you record, try to look past the imperfections and use it anyway.

**TEACHER VOICES**

Recording is awkward and uncomfortable at first, but I think there is great potential if you are willing to try.

—**Heidi Byer, fourth-grade teacher**

## *Focusing on Why You're Recording*

Recording and sharing are easy. Teaching is not. It is important to keep the why for recording in mind. You have already done the hardest part by preparing your lesson. Taking the step to record should reinforce that focus. Remember that you are not recording *yourself.* You are recording your lesson. Start with a tutorial or welcome video for your class. You can record it privately and redo it as many times as you feel necessary to capture the message you want to share. Before you begin, consider the guidelines in figure 3.1 as you establish and maintain this focus on *why.*

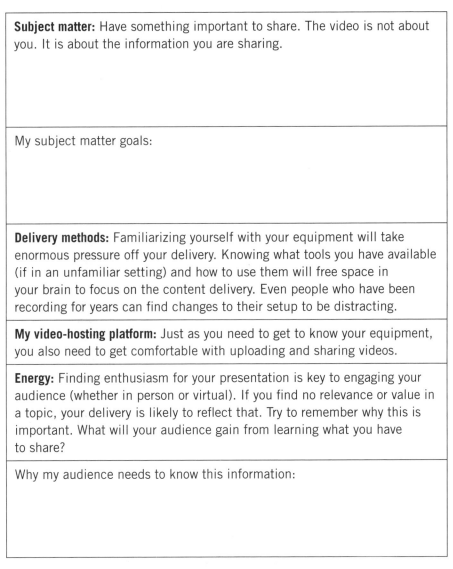

**Subject matter:** Have something important to share. The video is not about you. It is about the information you are sharing.

My subject matter goals:

**Delivery methods:** Familiarizing yourself with your equipment will take enormous pressure off your delivery. Knowing what tools you have available (if in an unfamiliar setting) and how to use them will free space in your brain to focus on the content delivery. Even people who have been recording for years can find changes to their setup to be distracting.

**My video-hosting platform:** Just as you need to get to know your equipment, you also need to get comfortable with uploading and sharing videos.

**Energy:** Finding enthusiasm for your presentation is key to engaging your audience (whether in person or virtual). If you find no relevance or value in a topic, your delivery is likely to reflect that. Try to remember why this is important. What will your audience gain from learning what you have to share?

Why my audience needs to know this information:

Figure 3.1: Focus on why you're recording.

*Visit **go.SolutionTree.com/technology** for a free reproducible version of this figure.*

### *Pressing Delete if It Doesn't Pass Muster*

An assignment might have changed slightly since the time of the recording, or maybe the principal made an announcement in the middle of the class you were recording. Maybe after reviewing your video, it doesn't seem particularly helpful to students, or you have developed a better way to make a point or found the perfect anecdote to drive the lesson home. Whatever the reason, roll with it. It's your archive, and you can update, tweak, delete, and rerecord whenever the spirit moves you!

**TEACHER
TIP**

Communication may be key, but appearance makes a difference, whether we think it should or not. What you wear has an effect researchers call *enclothed cognition*, referring to the way clothing affects our mental state and performance—and how other people perceive you (Adam & Galinsky, 2012). Communications author Darlene Price (as cited in Smith, 2014) explains it this way: "When you combine your appearance with communication skills, not only is others' perception of you affected, but their behavior toward you is also influenced. This will affect your students' perceptions of you, and vice versa. And while no teacher assesses students on how they look, you can ask them to think about how they feel when they are taking care with their appearance."

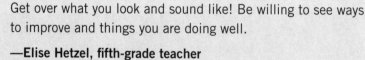

**TEACHER
VOICES**

Get over what you look and sound like! Be willing to see ways to improve and things you are doing well.

**—Elise Hetzel, fifth-grade teacher**

Creating videos is not a perfect art. You are trying to capture the classroom experience. It will not be perfect, but that is part of the charm and authenticity for the students. Do not spend a ton of time creating bells and whistles for your videos and instead focus on the content as that is what you want your students to focus on.

**—John Wilkinson, high school physics teacher**

## *Self-Evaluating and Getting and Giving Feedback*

Videos, of course, are not only a source of content for students to use for learning but also a place where you can look to develop professionally. That development can result from self-evaluation, as well as evaluations from colleagues and students. Whether you are asking a colleague to provide feedback about your video content or surveying students for video evaluations, others will have insights that can help you to improve your teaching *and* your video archive. Making the effort to ask students for their feedback not only makes them feel that their perspective matters but also leads to improvements in your teaching. How does this lead to confidence? The more substantive feedback you get, the better you are at *professional vision*, or "the ability of professionals in any discipline to make sense of the phenomena of interest to them" (Goodwin, 1994, as cited in Sherin & Dyer, 2017). Read more about these topics in the following sections.

- Self-evaluation
- Peer evaluation
- Student-to-teacher feedback

### Self-Evaluation

Assessing yourself by watching your videos can improve your teaching. Two researchers who have spent decades studying how videos impact instruction, Miriam Gamoran Sherin and Elizabeth B. Dyer (2017), explain that it's important to allow for the messiness of teaching instead of trying to only evaluate those that show seamless interactions. Instead of seeing what you have done wrong (or right), Sherin and Dyer (2017) suggest using videos to "learn to notice key aspects of classroom interactions that might otherwise be overlooked." Incorporating wait time (instead of immediately answering the questions you pose to students) is one example of something that is hard to notice about a class while conducting it, especially if you are new to using it (Rowe, 1986; Smith & King, 2017; Stahl, 1994). Much like how you want to keep the *why* in mind as you record, when you watch, continue to ask yourself, "What is happening, and why is this happening?" (Sherin & Dyer, 2017). Figure 3.2 (page 92) is a self-evaluation form for teachers. Of course, depending on your subject, these questions would change.

Beyond the self-evaluation form, ask yourself questions about what students specifically do and say in the video: What ideas did any one student present? Who was talking about a particular concept? How are students making sense of what I was teaching them (Sherin & Dyer, 2017)? Like the kind of higher-level thinking teachers want students to use, teachers will have to dig deeper to go beyond looking for whether students were

| Lesson and date: | | |
|---|---|---|
| | **Yes** | **No** |
| Was I audible? | | |
| Did the students appear to be engaged? | | |
| Did I use at least three seconds of wait time? | | |
| Did I adjust my delivery to the needs of my audience? | | |
| Did I frequently check on remote learners to ensure that they could see and hear the material and the classroom? | | |
| Areas of strength: | | |
| Growth opportunities: | | |

**Figure 3.2: Teacher self-evaluation form.**

*Visit **go.SolutionTree.com/technology** for a free reproducible version of this figure.*

answering correctly and instead seek insight into how students might have arrived at a certain idea, or how similar thinking between different students relates. They might ask questions such as, "Where do you think Zach may have gotten the idea that the slope was zero?" and "Do you think Hannah and Mateo are making the same point?" (Sherin & Dyer, 2017). Sherin and Dyer (2017) further explain, "These questions often lead teachers to develop new instructional practices based on the explanations they discuss. Further, we find that teachers begin to apply this same approach of working to make sense of student thinking during their subsequent teaching." Without video to review classroom lessons, these types of opportunities for discussion and analysis would not be possible.

It has been fascinating to see myself on camera. I have become more confident, and I have made changes to a few of my habits.

**—Heidi Byer, fourth-grade teacher**

I've really appreciated being able to watch myself and review my teaching. It also helps me be more succinct and efficient in my lessons.

**—Elise Hetzel, fifth-grade reading teacher**

Recording has opened up a level of flexibility to reach students at home and also, personally, to be able to teach remotely if the need arises. I've also been able to critically watch my lessons and make shifts and changes from the lens of a participant.

**—Angela McGuire, secondary special education teacher**

## TEACHER
### VOICES

### Peer Evaluation

I am a home-improvement TV show junkie. I love looking at houses, imagining how I would take out walls, add my own pops of color, and uncover hidden hardwood floors. When I watch these shows, my good-idea light is fully charged. Looking around at my actual surroundings, sometimes I can't see past a design feature that does not appeal to me. Those professionals on TV—if I could convince them to come for a walk-through—would know just what to do. Sometimes we need to see a situation through someone else's lens to evaluate it in a new light. Using video for colleagues to evaluate one another can lead to instruction makeovers (although you might have opinions about the classroom decor, too). Not only does evaluating videos provide the potential to gain feedback about your own teaching, but it gives you an insight into someone else's teaching style and environment, as well—that directly benefits students and educators (Ronfeldt, Farmer, McQueen, & Grissom, 2015).

This concept of peer evaluation is not new, but using video to do it together in a book-club style is an interesting spin on the old method of popping in to observe someone. Researchers who followed a video club of teachers who met, viewed, and discussed classroom videos of each other for two years came to the conclusion that the participation impacted the teachers' professional vision and that participation in such clubs "can support teacher learning in ways that extend beyond the boundaries of the video club meetings themselves" (Sherin & van Es, 2009, p. 20).

Working together to evaluate classroom videos brings more dimension to critiques from colleagues. One person may have a completely different viewpoint than another. This interaction can help teachers work together to make sense of what happens in their classrooms:

> They can consider alternative explanations for a student's ideas and for what the class might understand about a topic. . . . we encourage teachers to share examples of practice rather than exemplars and moments of confusion rather than clarity. (Sherin & Dyer, 2017)

How you approach peer evaluations can make a significant difference in the feedback you produce. Focusing on "one or two key skills" is more effective and less overwhelming than trying to tackle several areas (Frontline Education, n.d.). The tool in figure 3.3 offers structure to peer video evaluations, with two focus points: physical environment and classroom culture.

The rubric in figure 3.4 (page 97) is an adaptation of The Danielson Group (n.d.) framework for domain one. There are many samples on the internet that you can use to modify for your purposes. You are, after all, seeking feedback for your own self-improvement, so customize the rubric to suit your needs.

### Student-to-Teacher Feedback

Teachers know that giving students actionable feedback, both informal and formal, is best practice. What is less common is teachers seeking feedback from students. This practice can build a sense of community in your classroom. (Visit **go.SolutionTree.com/technology** for a free community-building Try This.) When students believe that their opinion is important to you, they generally provide honest feedback designed to improve the classroom experience. It's important to ask early in the term so you have time to demonstrate that their feedback is valuable by implementing positive changes. Students spend more time in your classroom than anyone else. They have insights that only they can truly provide because they have a unique perspective. While some teachers may fear that students would

| Physical Environment |
|---|
| Describe aspects of the physical environment that promote learning and engagement. |
| How does seating affect connections between students? With the teacher? |
| How balanced is the interaction between students and teacher based on physical setup? |
| How does the teacher ensure all students can see and hear everything in the classroom? |
| How does the teacher make necessary materials available to all students? |
| Where is there a growth opportunity? |
| Observation notes: |

**Figure 3.3: Teacher colleague evaluation tool.**          continued ▶▶

| Culture |
| --- |
| How does the teacher include all students? |
| How does the teacher loop in students who do not tend to participate? |
| How does the teacher ensure students can express their ideas and ask questions? |
| How does the teacher ensure student choice and voice and handle inter-student conflicts about those? |
| What, if anything, do you need more clarification about to understand? |
| Where is there a growth opportunity? |
| Observation notes: |

*Visit go.SolutionTree.com/technology for a free reproducible version of this figure.*

| Unsatisfactory | Basic | Proficient | Distinguished |
|---|---|---|---|
| The teacher makes content errors. | The teacher's understanding of the discipline is rudimentary. | The teacher provides clear explanations of the content. | The teacher's plans demonstrate awareness of possible student misconceptions and how they can be addressed. |
| The teacher's plans use inappropriate strategies for the discipline. | The teacher's lesson and and unit plans use limited instructional strategies and are not suitable to the content. | The teacher's instructional strategies in unit and lesson plans are entirely suitable to the content. | The teacher's plans reflect recent developments in content-related pedagogy. |
| The teacher focuses on right or wrong answers rather than evaluating meaning. | The teacher primarily focuses on right or wrong answers. | The teacher occasionally focuses on evaluating meaning. | The teacher primarily focuses on evaluating meaning. |

Source: Adapted from The Danielson Group, n.d.

Figure 3.4: Teacher evaluation rubric.

provide vengeful responses, in actuality, "even with any occasional intentional skew of the data . . . students still do a better job providing feedback and assessment than even well-trained administrators" (Ferlazzo, 2019).

I send a student-to-teacher feedback form a day or two after the end of the course. The experience needs to be fresh in their minds, but I also want to time it so that there is no implication that any response might influence grades (even subconsciously). Thinking back to my start-of-term survey, students' questions are often about my teaching style. Those can be difficult questions to answer, so now I ask it of my outgoing students: "How would you describe my teaching style to students who are starting this class next term?" If students believe you will share their answers with their peers, they tend to take the feedback seriously. Nearly every student who responds to this survey includes some version of *Mrs. Linnihan is super organized.* Figure 3.5 (page 98) works for elementary and secondary students who are providing feedback to the teacher.

**Directions:** Select the option that matches how you feel.

I can hear the teacher from where I am.

- ○ Strongly Agree
- ○ Agree
- ○ Disagree
- ○ Strongly Disagree

I can see the teacher from where I am.

- ○ Strongly Agree
- ○ Agree
- ○ Disagree
- ○ Strongly Disagree

I believe the physical environment encourages learning.

- ○ Strongly Agree
- ○ Agree
- ○ Disagree
- ○ Strongly Disagree

I feel comfortable raising my hand in class.

- ○ Strongly Agree
- ○ Agree
- ○ Disagree
- ○ Strongly Disagree

I feel comfortable talking to my teacher.

- ○ Strongly Agree
- ○ Agree
- ○ Disagree
- ○ Strongly Disagree

There is at least one other student in class I feel OK asking questions or working with.

- ○ Strongly Agree

- ○ Agree

- ○ Disagree

- ○ Strongly Disagree

My teacher cares about my learning.

- ○ Strongly Agree

- ○ Agree

- ○ Disagree

- ○ Strongly Disagree

**Figure 3.5: Student-to-teacher feedback form.**

*Visit* **go.SolutionTree.com/technology** *for a free reproducible version of this figure.*

## Build Confidence for Students

Student confidence can affect demonstration of mastery of course objectives. Over the years, I have had the pleasure of reading many of my students' college application essays. It is always astounding to me that a student that I view as confident, intelligent, and motivated once might have felt lost in the educational system. Some reveal stories of being mislabeled—with a learning disability or language barrier—when in reality, they were simply shy. They were so terrified to speak that they simply would not participate, and this is a problem that compounds because "shyness increases as speaking anxiety rises" (Oflaz, 2019). When lack of confidence impedes a student's ability to communicate, no real learning can happen.

Nearly every adult can relate to the awkward feeling of attending a party that is "not happening," so to speak. Whether the host has not selected the right music to invite guests to mingle, or the first arrivals are slow to start conversing, something is off. Once the magic starts—someone breaks the ice with a friendly story, the music starts jamming, or your best friend arrives—everyone seems to take a collective breath of air. Very few social creatures enjoy those awkward first moments. For students who struggle with confidence, class can feel like an awkward party that never really starts. But overcoming the confidence hurdle can set a student free to engage in learning on a level that allows him or her to demonstrate mastery. Investing in building confidence will have an amazing payoff for both teacher and students. The more confident students become, the more comfortable they will feel in the classroom.

Understanding the mindset of the students who struggle with confidence can help you to find ways to improve their confidence. One study indicates that "significant gender differences" exist in scoring self-confidence: "females had significantly higher levels" (Jabeen, 2017, p. 144). So what does this mean in the classroom? While everyone can benefit from extra confidence tips and support, there may be a significant difference in how much more male students might need.

In the next sections, I explore the following confidence-building strategies for students. When students are confident, they are more likely to engage in activities, getting the most out of the classroom experience; therefore, making the effort to ensure that students are comfortable in the recording environment may set a more positive environment for learning.

- Addressing body language
- Getting students familiar with recording
- Spotting anxiety
- Self-evaluating communication skills
- Self-evaluating presentations
- Letting students fidget

## Addressing Body Language

Amy Cuddy, a leading expert in the science of body language and the impact of positive body language on behavior, is my go-to favorite psychologist and has heavily influenced my teaching. As Cuddy (2015) explains, "carrying yourself in a powerful way directs your feelings, thoughts, behaviors and body to feel powerful and be present (and even perform better) in situations ranging from the mundane to the most challenging." Cuddy's (2015) research on *power posing*—wide feet, sometimes with hands on hips, up in the air, or behind the head—gives hope to the underdog and the introverted by boosting their confidence. The science behind Cuddy's (2015) experience finds that body chemistry literally changes after two minutes of striking a power pose like the one in figure 3.6. Everyone holds the power for change and confidence. All it takes is two minutes of body posture adjustment in private to reset body chemistry and inspire confidence (Cuddy, 2015). In my teaching, I hype this idea of power posing before I share it. I encourage students to power pose before anything evaluative in their lives: speeches, sports, musical performances, interviews, and more.

Figure 3.6: Cuddy (2015) calls this a Wonder Woman power pose.

## *Getting Students Familiar With Recording*

Students of all ages notice when something is different in the classroom. They are naturally curious when anything breaks from the normal routine. From an unfamiliar observer in the room to a video camera set up on a tripod, students will notice. The best way to smoothly introduce recording into the classroom routine is to make it as normal as possible. Having the camera set up and ready to go on day one will establish it as part of the norm for the room. When they walk in on the first day of school, students size up the room, taking in the full environment you have created: posters, furniture, five-foot-tall Darth Vader in the corner. Whatever your brand is, it will come across.

In the typical first-day-of-school routine, most teachers discuss classroom rules, expectations, and goals. Students may be curious about the camera, so demonstrate and discuss why it's there and what you will do with it. Mentioning the use of videos in the future without demonstrating how that will work on the spot may produce anxiety.

Begin recording videos early to create a comfortable culture with the camera (day one if possible). The less attention that you draw to the fact that you are recording, the more natural the students will behave.

**STUDENT VOICES**

> I like the idea of short, prerecorded lessons giving us instruction. All I really want is some lenience.
>
> **—Tenth-grade student**
>
> This video had the same vibe as being in class because it was shot in class.
>
> **—Eleventh-grade student**

## Spotting Anxiety

For some students, adding the element of recording adds a level of anxiety. I have known exceptional student leaders over the years who have opted not to run for a class officer position because they did not want to prerecord a campaign speech for broadcast to the student body. When I first tell students that we will be recording in the classroom, some have these same types of reactions. If a student has anxiety about speaking or recording, there are ways to help.

One of the common symptoms of the fear of presenting is actually a desire to hide (Cuncic, 2020). While this desire will not likely result in having to coax a student out from under a desk, the modern form of hiding (missing school to avoid a presentation, for example) is still very real.

Anxiety presents itself in a variety of ways. Whether they are working out a mathematics problem on the board or doing a lab experiment in chemistry, nerves can affect students. You want them to be comfortable while you are teaching, so being watchful can help you recognize the signs when teaching. The following low-, medium-, and high-level anxiety indicators list some of the novel ways students have attempted to hide from speaking in my classroom over the years. If students are showing similar symptoms, they may need additional support from you or someone else to overcome their fears. This applies to students in all grades.

These are some of the low-level-anxiety symptoms I have observed.

- Asking to switch places with someone in the speaking order on the day a presentation is assigned
- Asking to come in for extra practice outside of class period
- Silently rehearsing a presentation while sitting in the audience
- Asking to go into the hall to practice before delivering to the class

Medium-level-anxiety symptoms include the following.

- Asking to switch places with someone in the presenting order on the delivery day
- Asking to use the restroom and taking an excessive amount of time before returning
- Making statements such as, "Mine is really long, so I should probably wait until tomorrow" or "I forgot to dress up today, so I should go tomorrow"

High-level-anxiety symptoms include the following.

- Skipping school
- Claiming to have forgotten or lost essential presentation materials (notecards, visual aids, or the like)
- Making catastrophizing statements such as, "This is going to be terrible" or "Just give me a zero"
- Biting nails
- Having jittery legs
- Tapping feet or hands
- Removing and cleaning glasses

Research shows that deep breathing "and even sighing—brings relief to people" (Wells, 2020). Another expert recommends going across the room to throw away a piece of trash since "any action that interrupts your train of thought helps you regain a sense of control" or naming three things you see and hear, and then moving three body parts (Hughes, 2017). The most important advice may be to practice. Communication scholar and coach Preston Ni (2013) weighs in with some good advice: "Nervousness is our adrenaline flowing, that's all. It's a form of energy." By focusing on the content of the presentation, nervous energy can flow naturally into it, giving students a direction for their nervous energy. If they feel confident, they may feel less nervous. Faking confidence can be another way to overcome mild anxiety. Tipping off the audience that you are nervous will make that, rather than what you are speaking about, the focus.

Students can answer a series of questions, silently or one-on-one with their teacher or school counselor or social worker (Cohen, Opatosky, Savage, Stevens, & Darrah, 2021).

1.  "What am I feeling? How do I feel it?"

2.  "What is causing this feeling?"

3.  "What strategies can I use to make myself feel better?"

4.  "Has this helped me in the past? How did it help? How did I feel after?"

5.  "How can I use this strategy?"

6.  "Did it work? How do I know? Do I need to go back and try again to solve this?" (Cohen et al., 2021, pp. 129–130)

### Self-Evaluating Communication Skills

One of the best ways to guide students toward improved communication skills is to have them watch themselves on video. Often, prior to seeing a video, students' perceptions of how they have presented do not match how they feel when they see a recording. After seeing the video, they tend to feel far better about their work. This informal style of self-evaluation can improve their confidence.

This focus on public speaking and presenting is not solely for a public speaking class. Many state, provincial, and federal standards emphasize the speaking strand as one of equal importance to reading, writing, and listening. As mentioned earlier, the Common Core State Standards require collaborative work and presentations (NGA & CCSSO, 2010). The sample assignment and discussion participation analysis in figure 3.7 can work for students who are assigned to evaluate their own participation on a recording of a class discussion.

### Self-Evaluating Presentations

When students do presentations of any sort, it is valuable for them to reflect on the experience. Presentation skills carry throughout all subjects, from speech to history to shop class. The skills continue to grow, from elementary level to high school and beyond. Requiring students to view,

**Directions:** Each class member will present twice over five class periods as determined by the group. The first time for you must occur during the first three weeks.

Name:

| Assessment | |
|---|---|
| Item | Points |
| Full article PDF | ____ /10 |
| Cornell notes (Link to Cornell notetaking) | ____ /20 |
| Summary | ____ /15 |
| Group feedback (given on presentation day) | ____ /5 |
| Double-spaced one- to two-page reflection paper (due midnight day after you present) | ____ /50 |
| | ____ /100 |

| Roundtable Guidelines |
|---|

- Each table will consist of students who examined articles regarding a particular issue or controversy. The article's viewpoint does not have to reflect the student's personal viewpoint. Sometimes, articles will be intentionally for or against a particular issue; other times, articles might be objective.

- Each student should share a summary, response to the article, and any other observations regarding the article, including insightful questions and quotes.

- While one student is sharing, all other students are attentive. (Feel free to write down some basic notes regarding what each person says if you don't want to forget an idea you wish to respond to.)

- After a student has shared, others in the group may ask questions about the article, its credibility, its logic, the evidence, or other elements.

- After each student has shared at the table, you will engage in a brief conversation about the different viewpoints.

  - What did you find interesting?

  - What did you agree or disagree with, and why?

  - Why is this issue important?

  - What sources seemed biased, and how could you tell?

- Each table will summarize their discussion and the main points in the articles.

**Figure 3.7: Research roundtable student self-evaluation.**          continued ▶▶

- To prepare for each roundtable, you must do the following.
  - Print and annotate the text (longer articles can be annotated electronically) or take Cornell notes.
  - Cite the source using MLA style on a Google Doc.
  - Write a summary of the article beneath the citation (this summary may be changed to a reaction or discussion on occasion).
  - Include at least one direct quote. Remember to quote only something representative, original, important, scathingly brilliant, or that cannot be expressed in any other way.
  - Include your commentary. Explain the relevance of the article to your thesis.
- To write your summary and commentary, consider using a template. Writing a summary requires articulating a main point, relaying evidence related to that point, and avoiding bias (or pointing it out). Whether it is summarizing opposing arguments in debate, a scientific finding in biology, or a mathematical principle for physics, you will be asked to summarize ideas in writing in college.

| Discussion Participation Analysis |
|---|
| Name: |
| Note the times when you speak in the discussion, using the time stamp on the recording. |
| In the discussion, I asked direct questions about the following. |
| I asked this follow-up question to _____ (student's name) comment or question. |
| I directly referenced a specific quote (or page number or fact) from the reading. It was this. |
| I wish I had made the following comment. |
| I would have liked to talk and hear more about the following. |

*Source: Assignment adapted from Ryan Kramer, 2020.*

reflect, and write a self-evaluation is a way to promote self-directed learning and self-monitoring (Center for Teaching Innovation, n.d.a). Consider having students reflect on "how they studied or prepared, and what they might do differently in the future" (Center for Teaching Innovation, n.d.a).

To some students, the prospect of watching themselves on video is worse than actually giving the speech. Even though they get feedback from their peers and from me, the reality of viewing themselves often comes as a shock. Their perception of their delivery does not often match what most would consider the reality. Students may be convinced that they were swaying the entire time, or that the only audible word they mustered was "um." Watching the video forces them to face the facts. They are usually their own biggest critics. They would never harshly criticize their classmates the way they do themselves. That's another reason the self-assessment is so valuable.

One way to help students gain confidence is to require them to record their own presentations on their own devices and self-assess them privately (using headphones or in a quiet place alone, such as the hallway) using the form in figure 3.8 (page 108) for secondary students. The form in figure 3.9 (page 109) is for elementary students. This way, they know that they will be the only authorized viewer unless they choose to share the video. Of course, this requires students to have a personal device accessible in the classroom. If the formal feedback they receive from the teacher does not match their own perception of how the delivery went, the student and teacher can review the video together. While this is not the type of video you would save to your classroom archive, you may want to ask students to allow you to save them elsewhere as exemplars (and ensuring you get parent permission). Future students will benefit from seeing examples of an assignment when preparing their own. If students don't have their own phone or other recording device, you can record all student presentations on one device, and have students take turns watching privately.

## *Letting Students Fidget*

Some students need to fidget. Doing so intentionally can help students self-regulate ADHD, and "an effective fidget doesn't distract you from your primary task because it is something you don't have to think about" (Rotz & Wright, 2020). It does not mean the classroom erupts into pandemonium. Some students may not need to fidget at all. Not everyone who could benefit from fidgeting necessarily has ADHD, however. Fidgeting may calm nervous energy in students. As long as students do not disrupt others, it is an option if they feel it will help them. If the fidgeting becomes distracting,

| | Yes | No |
|---|---|---|
| Name:<br>Date: | | |
| Speech title or assignment: | | |
| Did I make eye contact with my audience during my speech? | | |
| Was I audible? | | |
| Did my audience appear to be engaged? | | |
| Did I adjust my delivery to the needs of my audience? | | |
| What was the best aspect of my speech? | | |
| On a scale from 1 to 5 (1 is not at all effective and 5 is as effective as possible), how effective was my visual? Please explain your answer. | | |
| What kind of visual or audio would have made my speech better?<br>In what way? | | |
| On a scale from 1 to 5 (1 is least comfortable and 5 is totally comfortable), how comfortable did I feel in front of the class? | | |
| What do I want to improve in my speaking skills? | | |
| What could I have done better when trying to convey my point? | | |
| How proficient was I in showing the assigned skill or topic? | | |

**Figure 3.8: Presentation self-evaluation form.**

*Visit **go.SolutionTree.com/technology** for a free reproducible version of this figure.*

| |
|---|
| Name: |
| **Directions:** Select the answer that matches your answer. |

I was loud enough.

   ○ Strongly Agree

   ○ Agree

   ○ Disagree

   ○ Strongly Disagree

I looked my teacher in the eyes.

   ○ Strongly Agree

   ○ Agree

   ○ Disagree

   ○ Strongly Disagree

I looked my classmates in the eyes.

   ○ Strongly Agree

   ○ Agree

   ○ Disagree

   ○ Strongly Disagree

I waited my turn to speak.

   ○ Strongly Agree

   ○ Agree

   ○ Disagree

   ○ Strongly Disagree

I said everything I wanted to say.

   ○ Strongly Agree

   ○ Agree

   ○ Disagree

   ○ Strongly Disagree

Figure 3.9: Elementary student communication self-evaluation form.

*Visit **go.SolutionTree.com/technology** for a free reproducible version of this figure.*

you may want to limit it to the time between presentations or just to fidgeting out of view of the presenters.

Very rarely is the purpose of a presentation solely to assess a student's ability to present. The focus should be on the content itself. For example, a chemistry demonstration may assess speaking skills in a marginal way, but the primary focus of the grading is logically on the content of the experiment itself. A speaker with excellent volume is not enough to carry the weight of an experiment that does not produce the desired results. A product marketing proposal in a business class will require more than good eye contact and body language. It is the marketing strategy that is the central focus of the assignment, not the delivery. Placing the emphasis on the material rather than the delivery can naturally reduce anxiety. Teach students that they have control over their thoughts, sharing:

> *Rather than think, "I'm going to bomb," for example, say, "I'm nervous, but I'm prepared. Some things will go well, and some may not,". . . Getting into a pattern of rethinking your fears helps train your brain to come up with a rational way to deal with your anxious thoughts. (Chansky, 2012, as cited in Hughes, 2017)*

Offering opportunities for students to do a test run or submit a draft prior to presenting can also build confidence in the quality of their work. Some students will still feel nervous, even if the presentation is not a graded assessment, however.

Having a few tricks up your sleeve can help. Here are some of my favorite nervous-energy-releasing options. You may allow students to keep their own personal fidget items in their desk or have class resources. It's important that students see these items as energy aids, not recess equipment.

- Rubik's Cubes
- Paper clips (Stringing them together keeps hands busy and minds focused on the primary task.)
- Coloring pages (Yes, even high school students enjoy coloring occasionally!)
- Nail polish (This is perhaps my most nonconventional trick, but for some, it really works!)
- Building blocks

Whatever works for the student is fine, as long as it does not create a mess or distract others. A little physical distraction can go a long way toward putting the mind at ease (Hughes, 2017).

## Try This

The driving force behind anyone's fear of public speaking is likely a fear of being evaluated. If you can convince both your students and yourself that the presentation is about the subject matter and not the speaker, you may make a huge breakthrough. I recommend modeling a StoryCorps interview. This assignment incorporates so many essential skills, including speaking and listening. Students need to plan the interview, requiring executive functioning skills such as planning and coordinating with others. They need to consider the subject of their interview and prepare appropriate questions, and then be able to conduct the interview in a way that includes natural delivery and follow-up questions. Conducting an interview is a life skill that students rarely get the chance to try.

1. Go to https://storycorps.org, a website that has a free downloadable app. This app allows users to listen to previously recorded interviews, browse recommended questions, record, share, and archive an interview. (Visit **go.SolutionTree.com /technology** for live links to the websites mentioned in this book.)

2. Select and contact someone to interview. This should be someone you think will have interesting life stories that you could document. The site provides lists of good conversation starters for any type of interview.

3. Use the website's free app to record an interview. The interview is stored on StoryCorps's national archive.

4. Model the assignment by sharing it with your class. You may choose to play an interview from the archive that sounds interesting to the class as a whole or to share one that you have recorded personally.

After introducing the assignment to the class, share the directions and form in figure 3.10 (page 112). Students should interview someone with whom they feel they could conduct a comfortable and meaningful interview for a significant amount of time (between thirty and forty-five minutes for secondary students, perhaps five to ten minutes for elementary students). While this may seem long, the stories that the questions elicit require time. Again, the focus is on the subject of the interview, not the student interviewer.

| **Directions** |
|---|
| 1. Download the StoryCorps app on your phone or go to https://storycorps.org on your laptop. Create an account to participate. |
| 2. Choose someone to interview and contact him or her. This can be a relative, neighbor, teacher, coach, or someone else. It should be someone that you feel has some life experiences that would be interesting to hear. (Choosing your best friend of the same age will unlikely produce any depth of content.) |
| 3. Check out the list of suggested questions on the StoryCorps's website (https://storycorps.org/participate/great-questions) so you are ready to lead the interview. |
| 4. On your scheduled interview date and time, record the interview on your phone or device. |
| 5. Share the interview with me. |
| 6. Complete the interview reflection. |
| 7. Turn in all materials. |

| **Interview Reflection** |
|---|
| My name: |
| My interviewee: |
| Relationship to me: |
| Date of interview: |
| On a scale of 1 to 10 (1 being certain you did a horrible job and 10 being elated), what is your overall feeling about how the interview went? |
| What, if anything, surprised you in this experience? |
| Why did you choose this person to interview? |
| Is there anything else you wish you had asked? |

| Is there anything you wish you hadn't asked? |
| :--- |
| What advice would you give to someone who might consider using the StoryCorps app? |
| In what way, if any, has this improved your ability as a public speaker? |
| What do you still want to improve in your own speaking abilities? |

**Figure 3.10: StoryCorps interview assignment.**

*Visit **go.SolutionTree.com/technology** for a free reproducible version of this figure.*

## Conclusion

Investing time in helping your students gain confidence in presenting will improve both speaking and listening skills. Confidence is the gateway to success in so many aspects of life, but some students need support to develop it. Recording and reviewing for self-assessment is a great way to improve student confidence. While some students (and maybe even *you*) will need to ease into the idea of recording their voice and image for others to see, the payoff is well worth the investment. Communication practice and confidence building set the stage for future success and empowerment, unleashing potential in a variety of ways.

---

[19]*Computer display with voice narration:* www.youtube.com/watch?v=FyFKbcK-J6I&t=1s

# EPILOGUE

Building a video archive isn't a process that requires you to jump feet first into it. It's OK to ease into it, getting a feel for what works for you and your students. When I started running, it was on a whim. I challenged my family to a run every night after dinner. We lived on a loop that was exactly one mile. At any given point in the run, no one was ever more than half a mile from home. For me, the effect of knowing that I could bail at any time and just walk home actually pushed me to keep running. In the end, only the goldendoodle stuck with me as I started to train for half marathons.

The point is that I never would have believed that I could be a runner when I started this family ritual. I was just trying to motivate the family to do something healthy together. I had a mantra that ran through my head: "You don't have to go fast. You just have to *go*." Every step I took was one step closer to my goal. Each individual step was easy. Looking at a run—whether it is a half mile or a half marathon—in this way is a great mindset to adopt for creating a video archive. While some people might want to jump right into planning for what may seem like a marathon, it's OK to start slowly—one step at a time! No matter how far you run, it is more steps than you take sitting on the couch. No matter how few videos you create, it is more than you had when you started. Whatever pace feels right to you is fine. You may find yourself swept away by it, recording more than you planned from the start. Be prepared for your pace to vary along the way. There may be days when it seems like a good idea to record nearly everything. Once you have a diverse archive, however, you may not feel the need to record quite as often.

Setting goals can make starting anything new more manageable. Consider using the checklist in chapter 2 (figure 2.2, page 57) to get started. Like any training program, you just need to take it one day at a time. If on my first day of training I had looked ahead to the final week of my half-marathon training plan, I might never have started. The reality is that you only need to do the workout for day one on day one. Don't worry about what lies ahead right now. Once you take those first steps, it is much easier to take the next one, and then the next. Just keep in mind that you are the one driving this initiative. No one is holding you to a timeline, so move at a comfortable pace and remember that everything you do along the way is designed to make both teaching and learning easier in your classroom.

Technology is amazing, but it can also be overwhelming. The potential to geek out (or freak out) on the tech side of recording is real, but it does not have to be complicated. Keep your goal in mind: improved learning opportunities for your students. No one is expecting fancy graphics or sophisticated recording techniques. Recording videos can be as simple as pulling out your phone. Don't let the potential for superior recording prevent you from giving it a go. Start recording with the tools you have. Just be sure to keep a charger at school so you don't lose battery power throughout the day if you are using your phone to record.

My final advice for you, should you choose to embark on this journey of creating a video archive for your classroom, is to keep it simple. If something seems valuable enough that you would want students to remember or learn from it, then record it. If you record, post it. Basically, if students can learn from a video, it is worth sharing it with them. It is also worth sharing with your *future* students. Just as running provided me many pleasant and unexpected benefits (like improved fitness and sleep), once you start on this journey, you will discover many improvement benefits. You will have more free time to become a better version of you (you the teacher *and* you the human being). Your students will benefit from the best teaching you have to offer. When was the last time you heard a teacher complain about having too much time to get something done? What teacher would turn down free help? Free help from someone who thinks, acts, and teaches just like you? Start small, but think big. What could you possibly have to lose?

Remember the old boundaries I spoke about in this book's introduction—those that had dictated my effectiveness, and how they had burst like a bubble? Go ahead and burst that bubble by building and sharing a video archive.

# REFERENCES AND RESOURCES

Adam, H., & Galinsky, A. D. (2012). Enclothed cognition. *Journal of Experimental Social Psychology, 48*(4), 918–925.

Aken, K. (2020, October). *How teachers use video lessons to help ADHD students learn* [Blog post]. Accessed at https://study.com/blog/how-teachers-use-video-lessons-to-help-adhd-students-learn.html on April 30, 2021.

Aspelin, J. (2017). We can recite it in chorus now! An interactionist approach to the teacher-student relationship and teachers' relational competence. *Classroom Discourse, 8*(1), 55–70.

Barack, L. (2019). *Allowing students to retake tests mitigates fear of failure.* Accessed at www.k12dive.com/news/allowing-students-to-retake-tests-mitigates-fear-of-failure/553641 on March 25, 2021.

Barni, D., Danioni, F., & Benevene, P. (2019). *Teachers' self-efficacy: The role of personal values and motivations for teaching.* Accessed at www.frontiersin.org/articles/10.3389/fpsyg.2019.01645/full on February 2, 2021.

Borowski, T. (2019). *The Battelle for Kids P21 framework for 21st century learning.* Accessed at https://casel.org/wp-content/uploads/2021/02/AWG-Framework-Series-B.9.pdf on May 1, 2021.

Bradbury, N. A. (2016). *Attention span during lectures: 8 seconds, 10 minutes, or more?* Accessed at https://journals.physiology.org/doi/pdf/10.1152/advan.00109.2016 on March 16, 2021.

Bruney, G. (2012). *The teacher-student relationship: The importance of developing trust and fostering emotional intelligence in the classroom* [Dissertation, University of Toronto]. Accessed at https://tspace.library.utoronto.ca/bitstream/1807/35096/1/Glenda%20MTRP%20Complete.pdf on April 30, 2021.

Buffum, A., Mattos, M., & Malone, J. (2018). *Taking action: A handbook for RTI at Work.* Bloomington, IN: Solution Tree Press.

Carmichael, M., Reid, A., & Karpicke, J. D. (n.d.). *Assessing the impact of educational video on student engagement, critical thinking and learning: The current state of play.* Accessed at www.readkong.com/page/assessing-the-impact-of-educational-video-on-student-5574297 on April 30, 2021.

Carnegie, D. (1962). *The quick and easy way to effective speaking: Modern techniques for dynamic communication.* New York: Simon & Schuster.

Center for Teaching Innovation. (n.d.a). *Self-assessment.* Accessed at https://teaching.cornell.edu/teaching-resources/assessment-evaluation/self-assessment on February 3, 2021.

Center for Teaching Innovation. (n.d.b). *Teaching students to evaluate each other.* Accessed at https://teaching.cornell.edu/resource/teaching-students-evaluate-each-other on March 17, 2021.

Chambliss, D. F. (2014). *Essay calling on faculty members to learn their students' names.* Accessed at www.insidehighered.com/print/views/2014/08/26/essay-calling-faculty-members-learn-their-students-names on December 22, 2020.

Chansky, T. E. (2012). *Freeing yourself from anxiety: Four simple steps to overcome worry and create the life you want.* Cambridge, MA: Da Capo Press.

Child Trends. (2018). *Parental involvement in schools.* Accessed at www.childtrends.org/?indicators=parental-involvement-in-schools on December 22, 2020.

Chuter, C. (n.d.). *The importance of social connection in schools.* Accessed at https://theeducationhub.org.nz/social-connection/#:~:text=Social%20connection%20is%20defined%20as,in%20a%20sense%20of%20belonging.&text=Rather%2C%20social%20connection%20expresses%20the,in%20their%20interactions%20with%20others on August 21, 2020.

Clement, M. C. (2013). *Hiring good colleagues: What you need to know about interviewing new teachers.* Accessed at https://doi.org/10.1080/00098655.2013.769930 on December 22, 2020.

Cohen, R. K., Opatosky, D. K., Savage, J., Stevens, S. O., & Darrah, E. P. (2021). *The metacognitive student: How to teach academic, social, and emotional intelligence in every content area.* Bloomington, IN: Solution Tree Press.

Cooper, K. M., Haney, B., Krieg, A., & Brownell, S. E. (2017). *What's in a name? The importance of students perceiving that an instructor knows their names in a high-enrollment biology classroom.* Accessed at https://pubmed.ncbi.nlm.nih.gov/28188281 on December 22, 2020.

Creative Bloq. (2013, February 15). *How to make a tutorial video.* Accessed at www.creativebloq.com/video-production/make-tutorial-video-2131915 on May 2, 2021.

Cuddy, A. (2015). *Strike a power pose—but do it in private.* Accessed at https://time.com/4134376/strike-a-power-pose-but-do-it-in-private on December 22, 2020.

Cuncic, A. (2020). *Do you want to be invisible and hide from people?* Accessed at www.verywellmind.com/do-you-want-to-be-invisible-3973933 on April 3, 2021.

The Danielson Group. (n.d.). *The framework for teaching.* Accessed at https:// danielsongroup.org/what-we-do/framework-teaching-0 on May 2, 2021.

DeNisco, A. (2016). *Standout school systems honored: 24 distinguished districts excel in leadership, special ed, and college and career prep.* Accessed at https:// districtadministration.com/standout-school-systems-honored on December 22, 2020.

Dickens, C. (2007). *A tale of two cities.* New York: Signet. (Original work published 1859)

Ellison, L., & Brdar, K. (2019). *The benefits of video-mediated instruction.* Accessed at www.edutopia.org/article/benefits-video-mediated-instruction on April 12, 2021.

Ferlazzo, L. (2019). *Response: Student feedback on teachers should be a 'part of more classrooms'.* Accessed at www.edweek.org/teaching-learning/opinion-response -student-feedback-on-teachers-should-be-a-part-of-more-classrooms/2019/04 on April 3, 2021.

Fernet, C., Lavigne, G. L., Vallerand, R. J., & Austin, S. (2014). *Fired up with passion: Investigating how job autonomy and passion predict burnout at career start in teachers.* Accessed at https://doi.org/10.1080/02678373.2014.935524 on December 22, 2020.

Fields, E. T., Levy, A. J., Karelitz, T. M., Martinez-Gudapakkam, A., & Jablonski, E. (2012). The science of professional development. *Phi Delta Kappan, 93*(8), 44–46.

Fountas, I. C., & Pinnell, G. S. (2012). *Guiding reading: The romance and the reality.* Accessed at https://doi.org/10.1002/TRTR.01123 on December 22, 2020.

Frontline Education. (n.d.). *Tips and strategies to improve teaching with video.* Accessed at www.frontlineeducation.com/solutions/professional-growth/resources/ten -strategies-to-improve-teaching-with-video on March 24, 2021.

Gagne, M. (2016). *Robots bring homebound students to class.* Accessed at https:// districtadministration.com/robots-bring-homebound-students-to-class on February 1, 2021.

García, E., & Weiss, E. (2018). *Student absenteeism: Who misses school and how missing school matters for performance.* Accessed at www.epi.org/publication /student-absenteeism-who-misses-school-and-how-missing-school-matters-for -performance on January 15, 2021.

Gedera, D., & Zalipour, A. (2018). *Use of interactive video for teaching and learning.* Accessed at https://researchcommons.waikato.ac.nz/bitstream/handle/10289 /12216/Gedera%20and%20Zalipour%20ASCILITE-2018-Proceedings-1.pdf ?sequence=2&isAllowed=y on June 16, 2021.

Georgiev, D. (2021). *39+ smartphone statistics you should know in 2020.* Accessed at https://review42.com/smartphone-statistics on January 31, 2021.

Golding, W. (2011). *Lord of the flies.* New York: Perigee. (Original work published 1954)

González-Morales, M. G., Peiró, J. M., Rodríguez, I., & Bliese, P. D. (2011). *Perceived collective burnout: A multilevel explanation of burnout.* Accessed at https://doi.org/10.1080/10615806.2010.542808 on December 22, 2020.

Goodwin, B. (2018). Research matters / The magic of writing stuff down. *Educational Leadership, 75*(7), 78–79.

Goodwin, C. (1994). Professional vision. *American Anthropologist, 96*(3), 606–633.

GoReact. (n.d.). *The ultimate guide to video in the classroom.* Accessed at https://cdn2 .hubspot.net/hubfs/2123109/GoReact_VideoGuide_OB.pdf on May 2, 2021.

Grimm, E. D., Kaufman, T., & Doty, D. (2014). *Rethinking classroom observation.* Accessed at www.ascd.org/publications/educational-leadership/may14/vol71 /num08/Rethinking-Classroom-Observation.aspx on December 22, 2020.

Hattie, J. (2015). *What works best in education: The politics of collaborative expertise.* London: Pearson.

Hughes, L. (2017). *How to stop feeling anxious right now.* Accessed at www.webmd .com/mental-health/features/ways-to-reduce-anxiety on April 3, 2021.

Jabeen, S. (2017). Understanding the wellness of students: A comparative study of self-concept and self-confidence. *Indian Journal of Health and Wellbeing, 8*(2), 144–147.

Jennings, P. A. (2015). *Mindfulness for teachers: Simple skills for peace and productivity in the classroom.* New York: W. W. Norton & Company.

Kaltura. (2018). *Fifth annual State of Video in Education 2018: Insights and trends.* Accessed at https://corp.kaltura.com/wp-content/uploads/2018/07/The_State _of_Video_in_Education_2018.pdf on April 21, 2021.

Kampen, M. (2020). *8 powerful ways to promote equity in the classroom.* Accessed at www.prodigygame.com/main-en/blog/equity-in-the-classroom on March 21, 2021.

Kraft, M. A., & Dougherty, S. M. (2013). The effect of teacher-family communication on student engagement: Evidence from a randomized field experiment. *Journal of Research on Educational Effectiveness, 6*(3), 199–222.

Maack, D. J., Buchanan, E., & Young, J. (2015). Development and psychometric investigation of an inventory to assess fight, flight, and freeze tendencies: The fight, flight, freeze questionnaire. *Cognitive Behaviour Therapy, 44*(2), 117–127.

McGrath, H., & Noble, T. (2010). Supporting positive pupil relationships: Research to practice. *Educational and Child Psychology, 27*(1), 79–90.

Mellon, C. A. (2015). *Library anxiety: A grounded theory and its development.* Accessed at https://doi.org/10.5860/crl.76.3.276 on December 22, 2020.

Miller, R. (2012). *Teacher absence as a leading indicator of student achievement.* Accessed at www.americanprogress.org/issues/education-k-12/reports/2012/11/05/40371 /teacher-absence-as-a-leading-indicator-of-student-achievement on March 29, 2021.

MindShift. (2015). *Slowing down to learn: Mindful pauses that can help student engagement.* Accessed at www.kqed.org/mindshift/39375/slowing-down-to -learn-mindful-pauses-that-can-help-student-engagement#:~:text=One%20 way%20to%20promote%20engagement,practice%20can%20improve%20 classroom%20discourse on January 29, 2021.

Mora-Ruano, J. G., Heine, J., & Gebhardt, M. (2019). *Does teacher collaboration improve student achievement? Analysis of the German PISA 2012 sample.* Accessed at www.frontiersin.org/articles/10.3389/feduc.2019.00085/full on January 3, 2021.

National Governors Association Center for Best Practices & Council of Chief State School Officers. (2010). *Common Core State Standards for English language arts and literacy in history/social studies, science, and technical subjects.* Washington, DC: Authors. Accessed at www.corestandards.org/assets/CCSSI_ELA%20 Standards.pdf on June 17, 2021.

National Governors Association Center for Best Practices & Council of Chief State School Officers. (n.d.). *Common Core State Standards for English language arts and literacy in history/social studies, science, and technical subjects: Appendix A— Research supporting key elements of the standards.* Washington, DC: Authors. Accessed at www.corestandards.org/assets/Appendix_A.pdf on July 6, 2012.

Newhart, V. A., Warschauer, M., & Sender, L. (2016). *Virtual inclusion via telepresence robots in the classroom: An exploratory case study.* Accessed at https:// escholarship.org/uc/item/9zm4h7nf on February 1, 2021.

Ni, P. (2013, May 14). *5 tips for reducing public speaking nervousness* [Blog post]. Accessed at www.psychologytoday.com/us/blog/communication-success/201305/5-tips -reducing-public-speaking-nervousness on November 8, 2020.

Offord, C. (2020, July 13). *How social isolation affects the brain.* Accessed at www .the-scientist.com/features/how-social-isolation-affects-the-brain-67701 on April 21, 2021.

Oflaz, A. (2019). *The effects of anxiety, shyness and language learning strategies on speaking skills and academic achievement* [Abstract]. Accessed at https://eric .ed.gov/?id=EJ1231642 on April 3, 2021.

Opitz, B., Ferdinand, N. K., & Mecklinger, A. (2011). *Timing matters: The impact of immediate and delayed feedback on artificial language learning.* Accessed at https://doi.org/10.3389/fnhum.2011.00008 on April 28, 2021.

Pew Research Center. (2019). *Mobile fact sheet.* Accessed at www.pewresearch.org /internet/fact-sheet/mobile on June 30, 2020.

Pulukuri, S., & Abrams, B. (2020). *Incorporating an online interactive video platform to optimize active learning and improve student accountability through educational videos.* Accessed at https://pubs.acs.org/doi/10.1021/acs.jchemed.0c00855 on April 30, 2021.

Ronfeldt, M., Farmer, S. O., McQueen, K., & Grissom, J. A. (2015). Teacher collaboration in instructional teams and student achievement. *American Educational Research Journal, 52*(3), 475–514.

Rosenshine, B. (2012). *Principles of instruction: Research-based strategies that all teachers should know.* Accessed at www.aft.org/sites/default/files/periodicals /Rosenshine.pdf on January 30, 2021.

Rotz, R., & Wright, S. D. (2020). *The body-brain connection: How fidgeting sharpens focus.* Accessed at www.additudemag.com/focus-factors on April 3, 2021.

Routman, R. (2018a). *Literacy essentials: Engagement, excellence, and equity for all learners* (2nd ed.). Portland, ME: Stenhouse.

Routman, R. (2018b). *Rethinking guided reading to advantage all our learners.* Accessed at www.middleweb.com/38836/rethinking-guided-reading on May 2, 2021.

Rowe, M. B. (1986). Wait time: Slowing down may be a way of speeding up! *Journal of Teacher Education, 37*(1), 43–50.

Rowling, J. K. (2009). *Harry Potter: The complete series.* New York: Arthur A. Levine Books.

Shakespeare, W. (1997). *The taming of the shrew.* In G. B. Evans & J. J. M. Tobin (Eds.), *The Riverside Shakespeare* (2nd ed., vol. 1, pp. 106–142). Boston: Houghton Mifflin. (Original work published 1623)

Shanahan, T. (2018, September, 28). *What do you think of guided reading for secondary school?* [Blog post]. Accessed at http://shanahanonliteracy.com/blog /what-do-you-think-of-guided-reading-for-secondary-school#sthash.53f7fyzg .dpbs on June 21, 2021.

Sherin, M. G., & Dyer, E. B. (2017). *Teacher self-captured video: Learning to see.* Accessed at https://kappanonline.org/teacher-self-captured-video-learning-see on February 3, 2021.

Sherin, M. G., & van Es, E. A. (2009). Effects of video club participation on teachers' professional vision. *Journal of Teacher Education, 60*(1), 20–37.

Shute, V. J., Hansen, E. G., Underwood, J. S., & Razzouk, R. (2011). A review of the relationship between parental involvement and secondary school students' academic achievement. *Education Research International, 2011*(915326), 1–10.

Sinek, S. (2009). *Start with why: How great leaders inspire everyone to take action.* New York: Portfolio.

Smith, J. (2014). *Here's how your clothing affects your success.* Accessed at www .businessinsider.com/how-your-clothing-impacts-your-success-2014-8 on June 29, 2021.

Smith, L., & King, J. (2017). A dynamic systems approach to wait time in the second language classroom. *System, 68*(1), 1–14.

Sparks, S. D. (2010). Districts begin looking harder at absenteeism. *Education Week, 30*(6), 1, 12–13.

Stahl, R. J. (1994). *Using "think-time" and "wait-time" skillfully in the classroom.* Accessed at www.ericdigests.org/1995-1/think.htm on February 3, 2021.

Superville, D. R. (2020). *Remote learning will keep a strong foothold even after the pandemic, survey finds.* Accessed at www.edweek.org/leadership/remote -learning-will-keep-a-strong-foothold-even-after-the-pandemic-survey -finds/2020/12 on May 1, 2021.

Tan, F. D. H., Whipp, P. R., Gagné, M., & Van Quaquebeke, N. (2019). Students' perception of teachers' two-way feedback interactions that impact learning. *Social Psychology of Education, 22*(1), 169–187.

Terada, Y. (2020). *Covid-19's impact on students' academic and mental well-being.* Accessed at www.edutopia.org/article/covid-19s-impact-students-academic -and-mental-well-being on January 31, 2021.

Thurm, J. (Producer), Dunne, C. (Producer), & Kleiser, R. (Director). (1976). *The boy in the plastic bubble* [Motion picture]. United States: Spelling-Goldberg Productions.

Tomlinson, C. A. (2019). *One to grow on / The autonomous teacher.* Accessed at www.ascd.org/publications/educational-leadership/sept19/vol77/num01/The -Autonomous-Teacher.aspx on February 25, 2021.

Tucker, B. (2011). *The flipped classroom: Online instruction at home frees class time for learning.* Accessed at www.educationnext.org/the-flipped-classroom on July 28, 2020.

Vega, V. (2017). *Social and emotional learning research review.* Accessed at www .edutopia.org/sel-research-learning-outcomes on January 30, 2021.

Vierstra, G. (n.d.). *Teacher videos: 5 reasons why making your own videos can help with distance learning.* Accessed at www.understood.org/en/school-learning /for-educators/empathy/teacher-videos-5-reasons-why-making-your-own -videos-can-help-with-distance on May 1, 2021.

Weissberg, R. P., Durlak, J. A., Domitrovich, C. E., & Gullotta, T. P. (2015). Social and emotional learning: Past, present, and future. In J. A. Durlak, C. E. Domitrovich, R. P. Weissberg, & T. P. Gullotta (Eds.), *Handbook of social and emotional learning: Research and practice* (pp. 3–19). New York: Guilford Press.

Wells, D. (2020). *Anxiety: Breathing problems and exercises.* Accessed at www .healthline.com/health/anxiety/anxiety-breathing on April 3, 2021.

Wyttenbach, R. A. (2015). *Documenting laboratory procedures with video.* Accessed at www.ncbi.nlm.nih.gov/pmc/articles/PMC4521728 on April 10, 2021.

Zeiser, K., Scholz, C., & Cirks, V. (2018). *Maximizing student agency: Implementing and measuring student-centered learning practices.* Accessed at https://files.eric .ed.gov/fulltext/ED592084.pdf on January 29, 2021.

# INDEX

**#**

21st century skills, 13

**A**

absences and video archive use, 10–13, 14–15

accommodations, example of, 2–3

administration, getting permission from, 54–55

anxiety

    communication confidence and, 102–104

    fidgeting and, 110

    organizing tech tips and, 58

    shyness and, 99

    social isolation and, 10

AnyList app, 56

appearance/physical appearance, 90

Archibald, A., 47

archives. *See also* videos, types of

    about, 23–24

    benefits for students, 5–14

    benefits for teachers, 14–21

    filing systems and, 77–78

    laying the groundwork for, 75–82

    permission from administration and, 54

    professional growth, using videos for, 49

    recording different types of videos, 24–42

    recording specific subjects and approaches, 42–48

    steps to create, 3

    Teacher Tip for, 49

    Try This, 50–51

    why and how of, 4–5

assessments

    benefits of video archives and, 9–10

review sessions and, 35

supplemental or enrichment lessons and, 40

assignment instruction videos, 28–29

attention deficit hyperactivity disorder (ADHD)

fidgeting and, 107, 110

video archives and, 5, 8–9

audiobooks, use of, 36–37

auditory learners, 5

autism and benefits of video archives, 8–9

## B

Barni, D., 86

benefits of video archives for students

about, 5–14

absences and, 10–12, 12–13

attention deficit hyperactivity disorder and autism and, 8–9

content review and assessments and, 9–10

homebound students and, 12–13

instruction speed and, 7–8

public speaking and communication skills and, 13–14

remote teaching and learning and, 14

study tools and, 9

benefits of video archives for teachers

about, 14–21

collaboration and, 19–20

equity and, 16

observation ability and, 17–18

perspective on student viewing habits, 20–21

self- and peer evaluation and, 16

time saving and, 18–19

Benevene, P., 86

body language, 100, 101

Buchanan, E., 87

building communication confidence. *See also* communication

about, 85

anxiety and, 102–104

body language and, 100

building confidence for students, 99–110

building confidence for teachers, 85–97

deleting recordings and, 90

familiarity with recording and, 101–102

fidgeting and, 107, 110

focusing on why you're recording, 89

self-evaluating communication skills and, 104

self-evaluating presentations and, 104, 107

self-evaluation and feedback and, 91–97

starting small, 87–88

Try This, 111

## C

calendars

communication platforms and, 58–59

sample calendar page, 68

sharing, 67, 69

Canvas, use of, 19, 59, 67, 69

Carnegie, D., 13

checklists

checklist for start of term, 57

classroom recording checklists, 75

and preparing before the students arrive, 56–57

welcome video and communication email checklist, 67

chronic absences, 10. *See also* absences and video archive use

Cirks, V., 11

class setup, possible classroom setup, 26

close reading, 33–34

collaboration, 19–20

communication. *See also* building communication confidence

benefits of video archives and, 13–14

communicating with students, parents, and guardians, 63–71

communication platforms, 58–59

establishing boundaries, 64–65

self-evaluating communication skills and, 104

welcome video and communication email checklist, 67

Cuddy, A., 100

## D

Danioni, F., 86

deep breathing, 103

digital native students, 17

Doty, D., 20

Dyer, E., 16, 91, 92–93

## E

EDpuzzle, 42

enhancement tutorial videos, 30–32

enrichment lesson videos, 40–42

equipment
    gathering and preparing, 71, 73–75
    handmade tablet holder for overhead recording, 44
equity
    attention deficit hyperactivity disorder and autism, access for, 8–9
    benefits of video archives and, 16
evaluations. *See also* peer evaluations; self-evaluations
    benefits of video archives and, 16
    building communication confidence for teachers and, 86
    teacher colleague evaluation tool, 95–96
    teacher evaluation form, 97

## F

FaceTime, use of, 1, 2
FAQs, setting up, 61–63
fear, 87
feedback
    benefits of video archives and, 18
    self-evaluations and, 91–97
    student-to-teacher feedback, 94, 97, 98–99
females and confidence, 100
fidgeting, 107, 110
filing systems
    example folder and subfolder organization, 79
    and laying the groundwork for an archive, 77–78
    special-occasion files, 79–82
    Teacher Tip for, 78
five-minute videos, 30-32, 50–51, 74
flipped classroom, 5
formatting features, Teacher Tip for, 78
Four Corners activity, 26–27

## G

Google, use of, 18, 19, 59, 69, 74
grading and supplemental/enrichment lessons, 40
Grimm, E., 20
guardians, communicating with, 63–71. *See also* parents

## H

Hickman, A., 45
hiding, 102
homebound students, 12–13

hyperlinks
    document with links, 80, 81
    enhancement tutorials and, 31, 32
    instruction speed and, 7
    Teacher Tip for, 56

## I

instruction
    adjusting speed of, 7–8
    traditional instruction and video archives, 5
interactive videos, 42

## K

Kaufman, T., 20

## L

Lan, J., 47
learning management systems (LMS)
    benefits of video archives and, 19
    saving files and, 59, 76
library-use skills, 29
*Literacy Essentials: Engagement, Excellence, and Equity for All Learners*
    (Routman), 33

## M

Maack, D., 87
males and confidence, 100
Mann, M., 47
microphones, 25, 47, 74. *See also* equipment
music and theater videos, 45–46

## N

Nellis, J., 48
nervous-energy–releasing options, 110
Ni, P., 103
nonverbal cues, 18

## O

observations
    benefits of video archives and, 17–18
    sharing video archives and, 20

## P

Pandemic Perspective
    communicating with students, parents, and guardians and, 65
    laying the groundwork for an archive and, 76
    review sessions and, 38
    tutorial videos and, 30
parents and guardians
    communicating with, 63–71
    communication platforms and, 58–59
    permissions and, 54
    welcome videos/communication and, 66
peer evaluations. *See also* evaluations
    benefits of video archives and, 16
    self-evaluation and feedback and, 93–94
    teacher colleague evaluation tool, 95–96
peers and social connections, 12
permissions
    future educational use and, 69
    getting permission from administration, 54–55
    review sessions and, 35
    Teacher Tip for, 56
    teacher-led close text reading videos and, 33
    video recording permission form, 55
    in welcome video and communication email checklist, 67
physical education
    links to exercise demonstrations, 49
    recording specific subjects and approaches, 48
playback speed, 6, 7
PlayPosit, 42
power posing, 100, 101
preparing before students arrive
    about, 53–54
    archives, laying the groundwork for, 75–82
    checklists and, 56–57
    communicating with students, parents, and guardians, 63–71
    communication platforms and, 58–59
    equipment and technology and, 71, 73–75
    FAQs, setting up, 61–63
    permission from administration and, 54–55
    Try This, 82
    video-hosting platforms and, 61

Price, D., 90

professional development, 49

Pronley, D., 42

public speaking

    benefits of video archives and, 13–14

    focus on subject matter and, 111

    self-evaluating communication skills and, 104

## Q

QR codes

    chapter reading, 34

    choir and orchestra concert, 45

    computer display with voice narration, 87

    conducting band, 46

    debate instruction, 29

    enhancement tutorial, 31

    FAQ, 62

    five-minute video: literary analysis, 50

    group presentation, 39

    lecture, 38

    Mandarin Chinese language lesson, 47

    PE tutorial, 48

    physics enrichment, 31

    thesis statement instruction, 29

    tutorial: organizing and sharing a welcome video, 80

    tutorial: using week at a glance, 59

    tutorial: writing on a PDF, 76

    use of, 21, 22

    welcome, 66

    whole-class review session, 35

questions/setting up FAQs, 61–63

## R

Ramthun, M., 46

recording different types of videos. *See* videos, types of

recording specific subjects and approaches. *See* subject specific videos

remote teaching and learning

    benefits of video archives and, 14

    students' at-home technology logistics and, 70–71

review sessions

    benefits of video archives and, 9–10

    Pandemic Perspective and, 38

    recording different types of videos and, 35–37

Rosenshine, B., 9

Routman, R., 33

## S

scaffolding, 7

Scholz, C., 11

sciences and other lab-based class videos, 47–48

screencast, 35

Screencastify, use of, 32, 50, 74, 87

Screencast-O-Matic, use of, 9

self-doubt, 29

self-efficacy, 86

self-evaluations. *See also* evaluations

    benefits of video archives and, 16

    feedback and, 91–93

    peer evaluations and, 93–94

    self-evaluating communication skills, 104, 105–106, 109

    self-evaluating presentations, 104, 107, 108

    teacher self-evaluation form, 92

self-management, 6

Shanahan, T., 33

sharing video archives, 3, 19–20

Sherin, M., 16, 91, 92–93

shyness, 99

Sinek, S., 4

SMART boards, use of, 35

smartphones

    equipment and technology and, 73

    using QR codes, 22

    whole-class discussion videos and, 25

social connections, 12

social media and communication boundaries, 64–65

special-occasion files, 79–82. *See also* filing systems

StoryCorps interview assignments, 111, 112–113

student presentation videos, 39

students. *See also* benefits of video archives for students

    building communication confidence for, 99–110

    communicating with, 63–71

    communication platforms and, 58–59

    digital native students, 17

    familiarity with recording and, 101–102

    at-home technology logistics, 70–71

student-to-teacher feedback, 94, 97, 98–99

teacher-student relationships, 12, 53

welcome videos/communication and, 66

subject-specific videos. *See also* videos, types of

about recording, 42–43

music and theater, 45–46

physical education, 48

sciences and other lab-based classes, 47–48

visual arts, 42–44

world languages, 47

supplemental or enrichment lesson videos, 40–42

## T

teacher-led close text reading videos, 33–34

teachers. *See also* benefits of video archives for teachers

building communication confidence for, 85–97

student-to-teacher feedback, 94, 97, 98–99

teacher absences, 14–15

teacher-student relationships, 12, 53

tech tips, Teacher Tip for, 57–58

technical clarity and connectivity survey, 72

technology

equipment and, 71, 73–75

students' at-home technology logistics, 70–71

technical clarity and connectivity survey, 72

technology coordinators on campus, 71

time saving

benefits of video archives and, 18–19

five-minute videos, 30–32, 50–51, 74

traditional instruction, 5

Tucker, B., 30–31

tutorial videos

computer-screen–only tutorials, 87–88

enhancement tutorials, 30–32

## V

video archives. *See* archives

video cameras, 73, 74. *See also* equipment

videos

communicating with students, parents, and guardians and, 65–66

equipment and technology and, 73–75

video-hosting platforms, 61

why and how of, 4–5

videos, types of. *See also* subject-specific videos
about, 24–25
assignment instructions, 28–29
enhancement tutorials, 30–32
interactivity and, 42
lectures, 38
recording guidelines, 24
review sessions, 35–37
student presentations, 39
supplemental or enrichment lessons, 40–42
Teacher Tip for, 25
teacher-led close text reading, 33–34
whole-class discussions, 25–28
viewing habits, insider perspective on, 20–21
Vimeo, use of, 19, 61
visual arts, videos for, 42–44

## W

week at a glance
communication platforms and, 58–59
QR codes, 59
sharing, 67, 69
Teacher Tip for, 64
week-at-a-glance template, 60
welcome videos
and introducing video use, 65–66
QR codes for, 66, 80
welcome video and communication email checklist, 67
whole-class discussion videos, 25–28
world languages, videos for, 47
Wyttenbach, R., 47

## Y

Young, J., 87
YouTube, use of, 19, 61, 74

## Z

Zeiser, K., 11
Zoom, use of, 61, 87

### The Metacognitive Student
*Richard K. Cohen, Deanne Kildare Opatosky,*
*James Savage, Susan Olsen Stevens, and Edward P. Darrah*
What if there were one strategy you could use to support students academically, socially, and emotionally? It exists—and it's simple, straightforward, and practical. Dive deep into structured SELf-questioning and learn how to empower students to develop into strong, healthy, and confident thinkers.
**BKF954**

### Harnessing Technology for Deeper Learning
*Scott McLeod and Julie Graber*
Reshape technology integration in classrooms to build truly transformative learning spaces. This reader-friendly guide outlines a clear approach for properly and skillfully using digital tools to promote deeper personalized learning across subjects and grade levels.
**BKF728**

### Creating the Anywhere, Anytime Classroom
*Casey Reason, Lisa Reason, and Crystal Guiler*
Discover the steps K–12 educators must take to facilitate online learning and maximize student growth using digital tools. Each chapter includes suggestions and examples tied to pedagogical practices associated with learning online, so you can confidently engage in the best practices with your students.
**BKF772**

### NOW Classrooms Series
This practical series presents classroom-tested lessons that teachers and instructional coaches can rely on to engage students in active learning and problem solving. Use these lessons, which are grounded in the essential four C skills (communication, collaboration, critical thinking, and creativity), to connect technology to key learning outcomes and prepare learners to succeed in the 21st century.
**BKF797, BKF798, BKF799, BKF800, BKF801**

## Solution Tree | Press
a division of
Solution Tree

Visit SolutionTree.com or call 800.733.6786 to order.

# Wait! Your professional development journey doesn't have to end with the last pages of this book.

We realize improving student learning doesn't happen overnight. And your school or district shouldn't be left to puzzle out all the details of this process alone.

**No matter where you are on the journey, we're committed to helping you get to the next stage.**

Take advantage of everything from **custom workshops** to **keynote presentations** and **interactive web and video conferencing**. We can even help you develop an action plan tailored to fit your specific needs.

*Let's get the conversation started.*

Call 888.763.9045 today.

SolutionTree.com